CONGRESSIONAL REFORM IN THE SEVENTIES

CONGRESSIONAL REFORM IN THE SEVENTIES

Leroy N. Rieselbach
Indiana University

GENERAL LEARNING PRESS
250 James Street
Morristown, New Jersey 07960

Manufactured in the United States of America.

Published simultaneously in Canada.

Library of Congress Catalog Card Number 76-22306

ISBN 0-382-18271-5

Preface

CONGRESS IS A MUCH MALIGNED INSTITUTION.

It has been argued that the national legislature has ceded its powers, sometimes inadvertently and sometimes voluntarily, to the President and the executive branch, that Congress has lost its independent authority. Indeed, there is much to be said for this view. In the decades since the New Deal, the oft-quoted aphorism that "the President proposes and Congress disposes" has been true most of the time. Surely the chief executive has dominated national politics, setting the policy agenda for the nation and chiding the legislature when it is slow to respond to his initiatives.

This book proposes some variations on this theme. First, it suggests why Congress has preferred to respond and react rather than to initiate public policy. But, second, it also suggests that beneath this surface deference there have been some undercurrents of independence. Beginning with the Legislative Reorganization Act of 1970 some ripples of reform appeared. In 1974, in the wake of Watergate, the ripples became a floodtide. The latter part of the book focuses on whether the tide of reform continues to flow, altering permanently the position of the legislative branch in national policy making, or whether it is ebbing, restoring the executive branch to its position of dominance. Several visions of Congress in the future, particularly a Congress in which deliberation and active, effective policy making would be fused, are explored.

Discussion of such a Congress helps to make explicit the questions raised forcefully in the 1970s by Vietnam and Watergate about the future of America. Can the nation afford to permit executive bureaucracy to dominate the formulation of public policy? Are there reasonable and responsible ways to harness administrative expertise to the "public good?" Or, from the legislative vantage point, are there clear channels through which the voices of individuals, alone or in organized groups, can be heard? Can Congress, on behalf of the public, exert policy influence over a powerful presidency? Or, most basically, is there some way to create a governmental system capable of both solving problems and of responding to the needs and preferences of its citizens? Perhaps there are no answers to these questions, but the more they are debated and discussed, the more clearly we will perceive where the nation stands and what its future holds.

Leroy N. Rieselbach

Contents

CONGRESSIONAL REFORM IN THE SEVENTIES

Introduction

THE WAR IN INDOCHINA, THE WATERGATE burglary and cover-up, and the elections of 1972 and 1974 seem, at first glance, to have little in common. Yet their combined occurrence has set the stage for the first serious reform movement in the United States Congress in nearly three decades. These events have demonstrated once and for all that the modern liberals' faith in the ultimate benevolence of the American President has been misplaced. In addition, they have created both the climate and the commitment for a complete reexamination of the relationship between the two elected branches of our national government, a reassessment that has led many observers to conclude that the legislative branch must operate as a more effective check on the executive.

The Vietnamese conflict illustrated congressional impotence in foreign affairs. American involvement, as John Kennedy and Lyndon Johnson engineered it, and disengagement, as Richard Nixon conducted it, were almost exclusively managed by presidential decision. Only after Nixon became swamped with Watergate and related matters did Congress act to cut off funds for military involvement in Indochina. Similarly, most other aspects of the nation's foreign policy, especially in the areas of military strategy and defense posture, have been formulated beyond the purview of Congress; the President and the Pentagon have reduced the legislature to a minor role in world politics.

In domestic affairs the events surrounding Watergate illustrated a similar story. A President, without hindrance from Congress (even one controlled by his political opposition), engaged in or condoned numerous illegal activities: obstructing justice by concealing evidence of the break-in; using federal agencies—the Federal Bureau of Investigation, the Central Intelligence Agency, and the Internal Revenue Service—for political purposes; using campaign "dirty tricks"; trying to influence the judge in the Ellsberg trial; and temporarily accepting a surveillance plan that would infringe the civil rights of citizens.

A more general criticism of Congress is that it has not responded to national needs. Vested interests within the legislature remain firmly in tune with the status quo; the environmental crisis continues unabated; crime still abounds; poverty is, if anything, more widespread; millions are unemployed, and inflation constantly erodes the purchasing power of those who are employed. Congress has not responded to these crises, its antagonists assert, because it is not organized to deal effectively with contemporary problems; it has abdicated its responsibility, relinquishing to the executive the role of prime mover in public affairs.[1]

This decline of the legislature is neither inevitable nor irreversible. Congress still possesses the constitutional and statutory means to have a major impact on the formation of public policy. It retains the power to declare war and to appropriate money to sustain the military. It holds the power to authorize and fund major domestic programs. If it has not employed these powers, it is because most lawmakers have chosen, rationally or otherwise, to defer to executive expertise, to permit others to make decisions that they, as elected legislators, could choose to make for themselves. But reform is in the air; there are calls to "strengthen" the Congress, to restore its initiative in both foreign and domestic policy. Recent elections have made reform more than a possibility. A new breed of legislator—younger, less tradition-bound, more willing to experiment—has, temporarily at least, made its influence felt on Capitol Hill. Since 1970, these new legislators have taken a few steps, halting at times but of tremendous significance, to renew and reinvigorate the Congress.

Yet reform is often a siren's song, seductive in the short run, but fatal over the long haul. Reform, to make sense, must have a focus; reformers must envision a better state of affairs and seek to channel change toward that goal.[2] Contemporary critics have differing visions of American politics in general and Congress in particular. Some place their trust in the executive branch while others put their faith in Congress to bring about desirable political results. This book will explore some distinctly different views of what the legislature can or should do. It first suggests some criteria for evaluating congressional performance and then uses those criteria to describe the current legislature, to discuss recent reform efforts, to outline additional reform proposals, and finally to project a vision of one, perhaps useful, state of affairs.

Notes

1. This statement, of course, is an overgeneralization. Many legislators have been energetic and effective workers in the cause of social change and reform. As an institution, however, Congress has not distinguished itself as the source or proponent of novel solutions to major policy problems. Over the past four decades it has, with the exception of the early New Deal and the legislative initiative of 1964–1965, been found more often on the side of caution than action.

2. We must recognize that much reform is "politically" inspired. In seeking to bring about policy outcomes, reformers may try to alter the institutions held responsible for blocking the desired policy. Thus, in the 1930s frustrated liberals urged "packing" the Supreme Court with more justices to circumvent the conservative decisions of the "nine old men" on the Court; by the 1960s those same liberals were among the stoutest defenders of the liberal Warren Court. Similarly, the same persons who defended an "internationalist" President, Dwight Eisenhower, against crippling attacks like the Bricker Amendment became, a scant two decades later, the chief proponents of a congressional revival designed to impose limits on "militaristic" Presidents, Lyndon Johnson and Richard Nixon.

   The present essay attempts to avoid this sort of politically inspired reform. Rather, our attention will focus on changes that have been or could be initiated to bring about a vision of what Congress should become in the years ahead.

1.

Some Evaluative Standards: Responsibility, Responsiveness, and Accountability

IF EVENTS LIKE THE VIETNAM CONFLICT AND the Watergate affair indicate the need to rethink the nature of legislative-executive relationships, the issue becomes one of defining Congress' place in the national government. What should Congress do? Should it relinquish its claim to participation in policy making [Huntington 1973]? Should it focus its attention and resources on overseeing the executive branch, sounding the alarm when presidential leadership moves in the wrong direction or when bureaucratic performance is unsatisfactory? Should the legislature be content simply to represent the public, transmitting popular opinion to those who actually make decisions? Or should Congress revitalize its mode of operation and attempt to exercise policy initiative and leadership? There are three vantage points from which to assess Congress, all of which yield differing answers to these questions but provide a starting place for an analysis of the legislative branch.

The first perspective, the criterion of responsibility, focuses on problem solving. A responsible institution provides reasonably successful policies to resolve the major problems it is faced with. The emphasis of the responsibility criterion is on speed, efficiency, and, of course, success. Can Congress produce policy that deals promptly and effectively with national problems? If, as many critics of Congress believe, the answer to this query is "no," then reform proposals to improve the *product* of the legislative process are clearly in order.

The criterion of responsiveness emphasizes *process* more than product. This is not to suggest an indifference to policy, but merely to indicate that here substance assumes somewhat less importance than how the legislature operates. To be responsive, a legislature must listen to and take acccount of the ideas and sentiments of those who will be affected by its actions; it must provide an open channel of communication with those it influences. In other words, it must respond to the preferences of its clientele.

A third criterion is *accountability.* Congress can be held accountable; that is, its decisions are evaluated regularly by the electorate. If the decision makers are found wanting the "rascals" can be "turned out" of office. The contrast between Congress and the Supreme Court makes the point clearly. Justices of the Supreme Court, once appointed, are protected by life tenure and are virtually beyond any effective removal power; members of Congress must face the voters and can be denied reelection. Thus, the legislators must calculate the popular response to their actions (or inaction). In short, accountability operates after the fact: Decision-making failure may result in the loss of position and power should the voters conclude that new office holders would perform more successfully.

These three criteria of evaluation—responsibility, responsiveness, and accountability—are by no means mutually exclusive; they can be employed simultaneously. This is clear in the case of accountability. Regardless of whether we judge performance in terms of product or process, efficiency or representativeness, we remain capable of voting our legislators into retirement in the immediate future. Similarly, in the abstract at least, it is possible for decision makers to be both responsible and responsive; they can move rapidly, on the basis of full consultation, to adopt workable policies.[1]

In practice, however, there is likely to be conflict between responsibility and responsiveness. The stress of the former on rapid and efficient problem solving is at variance with the latter's concern for listening to a wide variety of viewpoints. To wait for numerous sentiments to be expressed may permit a problem to grow worse or to allow effective solutions to become obsolete. To act quickly while the problem remains manageable may be to prevent those whose views are hard to ascertain or imperfectly formulated from voicing their opinions. In short, it is unlikely that any institution can be fully responsible and responsive; there will be tension between these two evaluative standards.

In any event, assessment of Congress' place in the American political process requires some judgment about the degree to which one evaluative criterion or another should dominate the assessment. The reform proposals favored will depend, to a considerable extent, on which vision of Congress each person holds. Is Congress to be preeminently a responsible policy maker? Or should it give up its decision-making functions and concentrate instead on serving as a conduit for popular opinion? Or is it more important that the citizenry be able to hold its national legislature accountable? More realistically, perhaps, is there an optimum "mix" of responsibility, responsiveness, and accountability that will permit Congress to survive and to work well?[2] It is these issues that the remainder of this essay addresses.

Notes

1. Richard Nixon, in effect, made such a claim for his administration's handling of the war in Indochina. He argued that his 1972 reelection margin, in excess of 60 percent of the two-party vote, constituted a "mandate" both approving his conduct of the war during his first term and giving him *carte blanche* to proceed during his second. That is, he argued that he had been both efficient (solved problems) and representative of the majority of Americans (responsive). In consequence, he was reelected to continue such service.

2. Needless to say, this last possibility is the most likely outcome of any reform impetus. Congress would be unwilling to give up much that many of its members consider their legitimate prerogative. The issue, in realistic rather than utopian terms, is how to combine legislative functions most effectively, how to organize Congress most efficiently, so that the observer-critic's vision can be most closely approximated.

2.

The Contemporary Congress: A Critical Assessment

BEFORE SPECULATING ABOUT THE FUTURE, IT MAY be well to note the current state of legislative affairs. How well has Congress done lately? Baldly put, I advance these arguments: (1) *Congress has been*, at best, only *imperfectly responsible*; it has yielded much of its decision-making authority to the executive branch, especially in foreign relations. (2) *Congress has been modestly responsive*; it has listened but has done little or nothing to call forth less frequently heard voices. (3) *Congress has been held accountable far more in theory than in practice*, an unsatisfactory situation that is not entirely the fault of the legislature itself. If these propositions are true, and the evidence for them seems persuasive, then there is ample opportunity for reform. The legislature's performance can be improved on all fronts.[1] But reforms designed to improve performance in one area may have unintended and unanticipated repercussions on another front.

Congress' recent troubles do not seem momentary aberrations. Its basic structures have undergone only modest alterations in the past half-century. The 1911 "palace revolution" in the House of Representatives that overthrew Speaker Joseph Cannon marks the beginning of the modern era. From then to the early 1970s, with the single exception of the Legislative Reorganization Act of 1946, the main outlines of congressional organization and procedure evolved slowly, but surely, to the point where change has tended to be marginal.[2]

A DECENTRALIZED INSTITUTION

In general, Congress has become "institutionalized" [Polsby 1968]. Year after year many of the same people operate in the same setting using the same procedures. The congressional *modus operandi* is one of fragmentation and decentralization, with authority and influence widely, though not equally, dispersed among the 535 senators and representatives. Many legislators have a direct and immediate impact on some congressional decisions. In such circumstances, congressional politics becomes coalition politics. That is, proponents of various proposals seek, through bargaining, compromise, negotiation, or "logrolling," to assemble fragments of political power into winning coalitions. They try to mount sufficient strength, at multiple stages in the legistative process and in each chamber, to move a bill ahead, eventually to the President's desk.

The dispersal of power in Congress, which results in decision by bargain and compromise, is a product of numerous conditions. In the first place, the electoral process in America stimulates independence of central authority in those who win seats in Congress. Electoral triumph, especially in the smaller House districts, is almost always the product of the candidate's own efforts, with only modest assistance, if any, from the national political party organization. A candidate may have to survive both a difficult primary fight and a bruising general election struggle with the opposition. To do so, she or he will probably have to create the campaign's organization and design its strategy, raise the necessary funds, and put together an electoral coalition, all with little or no assistance [Kingdon 1968; Leuthold 1968; Hershey 1974; Mayhew 1974]. Given this necessity, most legislators pay prime attention to their districts, "where the votes are" and where the ultimate decision about their continuance in office will be made. Incumbents, having learned the ropes, begin their reelection efforts with substantial advantages over their challengers. Therefore, few sitting legislators are turned out of office, but a sufficient number lose every two years to reinforce the inclination of those who survive to court their constituents and resist national, centralizing forces that might jeopardize electoral security.

The internal organization, formal and informal, of Congress also sustains the individual legislator's independence. The specialized standing committees, the chief agents of decision making, constitute the major decentralizing force in Congress. The committees are relatively free of restraint; what they decide is often what the parent chamber will decide. To put it another way, committees are the repositories of congressional expertise; on each sit almost all of the legislative specialists on the topics in its area of jurisdiction. Nonmembers are prepared to defer to committee expertise, to accept committee recommendations. Of course, they expect reciprocal deference in their own areas of specialization.

The committee, then, is a highly independent body with substantial influence over legislative activity. Its chairperson, as the single most important member of the panel, wields a great deal of that influence. Chairpersons vary in the degree to which they employ their powers, but many possess the ability to shape what their committees do. Their ability to sustain their own views, or something close to them, within their separate committees, and the reciprocal deference among committees, noted above, make the fragmented, divided character of legislative authority clearly visible. In short, committee decisions are very often synonymous with legislative action.

The political parties in Congress, which might centralize legislative authority, are weak. The party leadership—the Speaker of the House, the floor leaders, and the whips—has few genuine sanctions with which to enforce discipline on the disparate party membership. As noted, legislators tend to vote their districts rather than the party line if tension between the two occurs. Committee considerations—the use of seniority to select committee leaders, the protection of the panel's expertise and power—often militate against supporting the party. Party leaders are not without some bases of influence, but the resources they possess rest on persuasion rather than compulsion. With these means, parties often successfully generate considerable discipline, but, on balance, they lack the power regularly and effectively to countervail the centrifugal forces that electoral and committee realities generate.

Congressional rules and procedures contribute directly to the fragmented, decentralized character of the legislature. The rules protect arrangements that require a bill to move past many "veto points," at which a bill must succeed or die. They define and defend committee jurisdictions, thereby serving to insulate the panels, to minimize the possibilities that they will be circumvented, and to guarantee that the major decisions will be made there. Among other things, the Rules Committee in the House and the rule of unlimited debate, the well-known filibuster, in the Senate help to buttress the position of legislative minorities.[3] These and numerous other intricate rules that might be cited make it clear that congressional procedures sustain a system of multiple centers of influence; in so doing, they contribute to the dominance of bargaining as a way to resolve conflict in Congress.

Finally, like any other organization, Congress operates within a context of mores and practices, nowhere codified but demonstrably observable, which color its activities. These informal traditions, or norms, foster a diffusion of power. Senators and representatives alike are enjoined to specialize in a small number of policy topics, to defer to one another's expertise, to treat each other courteously, and, in general, to behave in ways that minimize hostility and friction. This "legislative culture" permits the lawmakers to try to carve out for themselves a niche where each can eventually exert some influence over congressional decision making. Many are successful in this endeavor, content to possess a fragment of power even at the cost of achieving authority beyond their narrow focus of concern.

Congress, then, is a highly decentralized, fragmented institution. Electoral considerations, the committee structure, the formal rules and procedures, and the informal norms and expectations work to diffuse authority widely, though not in any sense equally, among the lawmakers. Many legislators become important in one area of congressional activity. Negotiation and compromise become the chief style of decision making in Congress; bargaining provides the only viable means of assembling the fragments of power into workable coalitions. The political parties, a possible centralizing force, have been incapable of overcoming the fragmenting forces. In consequence, and in the absence of other alternatives, the coalitional character of congressional politics has survived without serious challenge in recent years.

RESPONSIBILITY:
POLICY MAKING IN CONGRESS

Policy making becomes a slow, complicated process in a decentralized institution. To enact policy, those in favor must move their legislation through a subcommittee, a full committee, the Rules Committee in the House, and out onto the floor where a majority vote for passage is required. If the process can be repeated in the other house and all differences in the two chambers' versions can be resolved in conference committee, then and only then will some new policy, or modification of an old policy, be *au-thorized*. If money is necessary to implement the program, as it most often is, the entire process must be repeated, with *appropriations* legislation moving this time through the sub- and full committees of the Appropriations Committees. It is the need to move across, around, or over these imposing hurdles that gives congressional politics its distinctive, coalitional character. To assemble a winning coalition at each of these stages, and to do so in an environment where power is shared and the other legislators' feelings are respected, requires bargaining skill and patience that must be sustained over a considerable period of time.

Given this picture of congressional practice, it is not surprising that the national legislature has been judged deficient on *responsibility* grounds. To put it simply, Congress is not capable of acting with efficiency in any but the most unusual circumstances. Extraordinary situations do occur, as they did in the early New Deal period and during 1964–1965. On both occasions an exceptional coincidence of events gave the Democratic Party both the presidency and overwhelming majorities in each house of Congress.[4] Top-heavy legislative majorities make the weakness of party discipline tolerable and provide the dominant party with incentives to advance a major legislative program. But ordinarily conditions are far less favorable. Where partisan control of government is divided, with one party controlling the presidency and the other holding a congressional majority (as has been the case for 14 of the last 24 years), prospects for cooperative and inventive lawmaking are substantially reduced. The 1975 struggle over energy policy, which produced no meaningful steps to reduce domestic oil consumption, is typical of conflictual policy making under conditions of divided control. Even when the President and the congressional majority share a common party label, responsible lawmaking seldom follows, for nominal majorities show a decided tendency to evaporate when the roll is called. Thus, policy making in Congress flows from slow, painstaking negotiations, which often cross rather than follow party lines.

This policy making by negotiation is especially apparent in domestic affairs, where Congress retains much authority and the end result does regularly bear the imprint of legislative deliberation and decision. Congress seems to prefer to respond to presidential initiative, to demand that the chief executive set the national agenda. Congressional criticism is commonplace when, in the lawmakers' judgment, the President is lax in proposing a legislative program. Once that program is forthcoming, however, the legislators are more than willing to alter its proposals dramatically or to reject them entirely. Numerous struggles—against Richard Nixon's efforts to impound funds properly appropriated and to extend broadly the doctrine of "executive privilege" in order to deny congressional access to information, and against Gerald Ford's attempts to impose a ceiling on federal spending and to deregulate oil and natural gas—amply testify to the legislature's ability to resist and defeat undesired presidential initiatives.[5]

When Congress is prepared to substitute its own for the executive's priorities, it provides ammunition to those who criticize it on responsibility grounds. As suggested above, the congressional process is something less than efficient. To assemble a winning majority takes time; accommodations to many independent power-holders must be made. The critics point to extended hearings, lengthy sub- or full-committee "mark-up" sessions,[6] long periods of delay, and use of the filibuster as evidence of the legislature's inability to act decisively. These critics do not always recognize that time may be the essential ingredient in legislative decision making, that delay may permit action by allowing a specific compromise settlement to occur. Still, their basic argument is sound: Congress does move ponderously. Furthermore, the negotiated agreements that emerge, that can command a majority, tend to be modest in scope. Proposals for major change are often jettisoned in the search for a winning coalition; they must be sacrificed to secure the support of critical power-holders.[7]

In early 1976, for example, the Senate Public Works Committee sought to revive a public works jobs bill that President Ford had vetoed. In hopes of winning at least three additional votes—the margin by which the Senate had failed to override the veto—the panel scaled down the cost of the jobs program and eliminated another antirecession program about which the President had raised specific objections. Such adjustments in the content of the legislation occur more commonly before initial passage.

In sum, in domestic matters, where Congress' influence is at a maximum, the legislative output is neither radical nor rapid. Congress seems in no hurry to respond to interest groups or executives, but prefers to develop its own domestic programs in its own way and at its own pace. Those who see responsibility as demanding more efficient development of more imaginative and innovative programs find congressional performance unsatisfactory. In ordinary times, Congress seldom generates dramatic departures; rather it gives shape and substance to the ideas of others and does so over extended periods of time.

From the point of view of responsibility, congressional performance is even worse in foreign relations. Over a number of years the President has capitalized on several advantages—the commander-in-chief power, vastly greater resources of information and technical expertise, the Supreme Court's *Curtiss-Wright* decision that the President is "the sole organ of the nation" in international relations, and most importantly the recognition by Congress that its mode of conducting business is often inappropriate in the foreign sphere. For all these reasons, Congress has come to defer to presidential expertise in military matters. The Armed Services Committees have become, in Lewis Dexter's [1963] phrase, "real estate" panels, concerned with the management of military installations. They are content to leave the more critical issues of military strategy and procurement to Pentagon generals and White House executives. Diplomatic initiatives, such as President Nixon's rapprochements with China and the Soviet Union, have been executive in initiation and conduct. Tariff agreements are negotiated by the executive branch under broad congressional delegations of power, which the legislature renews and extends at regular intervals. Wars have come under total presidential control; in the case of the two most recent ones, Korea and Indochina, Congress supported the military efforts initiated by Presidents without invoking its constitutional right to declare war.

This is not to say Congress cannot or could not influence American foreign policy. Control over the purse strings permits the legislature, if it chooses to do so, to deny funds for executive policy initiatives. The increasing unpopularity of the Vietnam conflict brought forth numerous proposals to cut off money for military involvement in Southeast Asia. Only in the last days of American involvement in the war, in early summer 1973, did Congress succeed in forcing the President's hand at all. In June, the legislature tacked a provision cutting off funds for bombing in Cambodia onto a $3.3 billion Supplemental Appropriations Bill, enacted to enable the federal government to keep operating in the new fiscal year beginning July 1. President Nixon vetoed the bill and the House sustained his action, but lest the government go out of business, the President accepted a compromise and signed a second supplemental bill prohibiting spending for military purposes in Indochina after August 15, some six weeks hence, without prior legislative approval. On the whole, however, the substance of the nation's Indochina policy—from its earliest inception in the Eisenhower and Kennedy administrations to the end of direct American involvement during Nixon's term—reflected the policy choices of the chief executive rather than Congress.

Likewise, Congress could have, but has not, reclaimed the power to set tariffs itself or to designate some independent agency to negotiate trade agreements. The legislature has tried, with only modest success, to keep closer tabs on military matters by insisting that funds for weaponry be authorized on an annual, not a long-term, basis [Dawson 1962]. The lawmakers have given shape to the foreign aid program: They have made major cuts in the President's fund requests, they have reallocated money from military to economic varieties of aid, and they have denied aid to Vietnam, Cambodia, Angola, and (temporarily) Turkey. Yet the President remains central and Congress peripheral in foreign policy making. As Senator Adlai E. Stevenson III (D., Ill.) put it [*Congressional Quarterly Weekly Report*, June 28, 1975, p. 1349]: "Congress is . . . unfit to formulate foreign policy or to effectively oversee its implementation in all parts of a fast moving world." Responsibility for America's international relations rests in the White House, not on Capitol Hill.

The public tendency to focus policy responsibility on the President rather than on Congress seems, then, to have some justice to it. The legislature is not preeminent in policy making much of the time, and when it is, it is only after an extended period of deliberation and debate. Congress has not been the *responsible initiator* of public policy; rather it has molded and legitimatized policy originating most often outside the legislative chambers.

RESPONSIVENESS: REPRESENTATION IN CONGRESS

When the spotlight shifts from responsibility to *responsiveness*, Congress appears in a considerably better light. Its defects on one front become its advantages on another;

its vices become virtues. Specifically, the very openness, decentralization, and bargaining style of decision making that seem to critics to inhibit responsible policy choice appear in the light of responsiveness as admirable features of Congress. The slow pace of policy making allows time for those with a stake in the outcome to communicate their sentiments to the members of Congress. The multistage process of lawmaking provides points of access to legislators; it identifies the places where outside pressures may be brought to bear on the legislature. Congress has always been more than willing to listen to what nonmembers have to say.

To put it another way, Congress has ample opportunity, and regularly indulges it, to attend to messages from interested parties, including the President, interest groups, and the public. As noted earlier, Congress chooses to depend on the President to set its agenda; the legislature responds to executive initiatives. Moreover, the President has at his disposal a full arsenal of weapons that comprise what Richard Neustadt [1960] has called his "power to persuade." Specifically, the President can use his popularity and prestige to influence lawmakers; it is difficult for them to resist a popular and determined leader. He can argue on the merits of an issue, using speeches, press conferences, special messages, and generally his ability to command attention. He can call on party loyalty by shaping his appeals to partisan interests. He can deal with a congressional committee by sending his chief aides and experts to testify at hearings; by courting the important committee members, especially the chairperson and ranking minority member; or by accepting amendments in order to gain votes. He may seek to win over crucial individuals—committee chairpersons, party leaders, influential members—through personal contacts. If he can secure the support of these leaders, they in turn may use their powers to persuade their followers to back him.

In such situations, the President's persuasive power rests on his ability to do favors, to provide goods and services. He can employ his veto to the advantage of some legislator or in other ways use his influence over pending bills to assist whomever he seeks to persuade. He may also make use of his patronage power, offering to appoint political associates of a legislator to federal posts. The President can give or withhold election aid; he can endorse congressional candidates, pose for pictures with them, or make personal appearances in their districts. If he is highly regarded, such electoral assistance may benefit the local legislative nominee. While it is not clear precisely to what extent these bases of persuasion are used—bargains struck are not likely to be explicit or widely publicized—these advantages do enable the President to work, from a position of strength, to influence congressional decision making.[8]

Through these methods, then, the President will appeal to the full legislature, to specific groups within each chamber, and to single influential lawmakers. Whether or not these techniques of leadership are successful in putting his program over, there can be little doubt that Congress will listen to what the chief executive says. To the extent that his constituency differs from those of the lawmakers—and the differences between the President's "national" orientations and the supposedly more "parochial" perspectives of the representatives of states and districts have been widely noted—the President will introduce into legislative deliberations points of view that might otherwise not be heard or at least might be less forcefully expressed. Congress, in short, is responsive to the President.

The legislature is also responsive to the views of organized interests. Organizations do move in and about the halls of Congress, and the lawmakers are often deeply involved with group representatives ("lobbyists") in working for mutually desired legislation. This is not to argue, as do some observers, that pressure group activity is decisive in lawmaking outcomes. Indeed, the best and most recent evidence suggests that the interests do not call the legislative tune (and do not really pay the piper either); rather they work in collaboration with, and sometimes at the request of, sympathetic congresspersons.[9] They lend support to developing coalitions working to pass or to block bills as seems appropriate.

Lobbyists seek to establish and maintain free and open lines of communication with members of Congress in positions to help them promote their specific group's cause. Much of their activity is designed to sustain this access; they may, in fact, run service operations designed to supply information, assistance, and contacts to lawmakers working for the views they seek to promote. In return for such support, the lobbyists hope to retain the opportunity to "make a pitch" to legislators concerning their client's interests. The pressure group belies its name; it is more often a coalition partner than an irresistible force in the legislative process.[10]

Even this reliance on low-key tactics, on friendship and trust rather than bribes or threats, provides groups and their representatives with ample opportunity to present their opinions. They appear regularly as witnesses at committee and subcommittee hearings. They supply research findings and documentary evidence directly to relevant legislators or members of their staffs. Through such channels, group postures become known to the lawmakers, often at a time when their own positions have not yet crystalized. In some cases, however, the group provides only data that reinforce the legislators' existing judgments; it introduces no new perspectives. In any event, if responsiveness is defined as maintaining open and operative channels of communication, Congress is responsive, at least to organized interests.

And here is the rub. While the national legislature does hear and have the opportunity to respond to the views of well-organized, well-financed interests—such as business, labor, agriculture, veterans, and the professions—other less affluent interests may go unheard and unheeded. Access is unequally divided; communications links are unequally available. Because of the decentralized character of the congressional process, many groups will have some access, but some will have ties to important leaders while others will relate only to the rank and file. Some important interests—the poor, the blacks, and, until recently, the consumer—are inadequately organized. Lacking experience, money, and know-how, such interests may be unable to present their positions effectively. What the legislators hear, in short, may be far from the full story; their intake of information will depend on what messages are being sent as well as which communications they choose to listen to.

One other audience, the unorganized public, provides a focus for legislative attention. Members of Congress are not prepared to accept the executive branch or interest associations as the "voice of the people." They examine the polls to get a general sense of popular sentiment. They attend, perhaps more closely, to opinions of their own constituents, as expressed in conversations, in letters, and in local newspaper columns and editorials. Some, recognizing the imperfect character of these sources,[11] commission their own opinion polls; others rely more on intuition, on their sense of what their constituents believe. For most lawmakers reliable information about constituency sentiments is not available; they do not really know what the "folks back home" feel on all but the most dramatic issues of the day.

Yet there is considerable incentive to pay heed to constituents' views. The legislators must decide whether their actions will affect their reelection prospects. Before they act, if they have no clear data on district opinion, they will take into consideration local realities, including their own feelings—however emotional and intuitive they may be—about what their constituents elected them to do in general and what they would want them to do in certain specific circumstances. This ensures some policy linkages, though clearly imperfect ones, between Washington and the local communities.

On the whole, then, Congress responds moderately well to a variety of interests. The legislature cannot avoid getting messages, loud and clear ones in many instances, from the executive; indeed, Congress demands such communications. Interest groups also abound, using their access to transmit their views to senators and representatives; the legislators find those views helpful and may even solicit them. Lawmakers also feel the need to gauge local sentiment; they seek to head off possible electoral sanctions by taking citizen opinion into account. Moreover, the decision-making process in Congress contributes to this responsiveness. Its decentralization and fragmentation, as well as the slow pace that its bargaining style of conflict resolution imposes, guarantee access points and time to transmit messages. Congress can and does hear many voices during its deliberations.

Yet the national legislature is by no means perfectly responsive, completely representative. In resolving conflicts it necessarily must respond favorably to some interests and less satisfactorily to others. Beyond this, however, it does not hear all points of view. The President is a forceful proponent of his own program; his messages will reflect his bias, and he may resort to "executive privilege" to keep some information out of legislative hands. Not all interests possess access equally. Some can reach only relatively unimportant legislators and decision points; others, lacking funds and skills, remain unorganized and hard pressed to communicate their views at all. Individual citizens are often unwilling or unable to present their views; their apathy requires that legislators guess about constituent preferences. On all these fronts—executive, group, individual—congressional responsiveness can be improved, and these defects have become the targets of reformers seeking to enhance the responsiveness of Congress.

THE ACCOUNTABILITY OF CONGRESS

These same defects, especially popular indifference to the legislature, also go far to explain the fact that Congress is held *accountable* only imperfectly. Accountability, citizen control of Congress through the ballot box, requires several conditions if it is to function properly. First, those making the judgment, the citizens, must be aware of the behavior of those whom they are to hold to account, the legislators. Second, the citizens must have some views of their own, some set of desirable goals for which they expect the legislators to work. Third, if legislative behavior and citizen preferences do not match, there must be some way for the citizens to express dissatisfaction; they must be provided with candidates whose views coincide with their own. Such an alternative may be found in the primary of the incumbent's political party or in the general election. In truth, all these conditions are poorly met in modern America. Not one of them is much more than an approximation of reality; all three exist in but a small minority of instances. In the absence of the requisite conditions accountability operates imperfectly in legislative politics.

Because the prerequisites for accountability are seldom found, congresspersons can act free of popular check on all but the most dramatic and emotional issues.[12] In direct contrast to condition one, the citizenry is on the whole unaware of the major details of legislative behavior. Polls continually reveal that large portions of the population are unable to name their elected representatives. The complexity of the congressional process, with its myriad decision points, is beyond public grasp. Even the most public act, the roll call vote, is unknown to many voters. Moreover, legislators exploit the possibilities of a decentralized organization. That is, they can act in inconsistent ways, working against a bill in committee, but voting for it at the later roll call phase. Such behavior will allow them to be all things—friend *and* foe—to all bills, and immeasurably complicates the citizen's task of understanding congressional politics. Finally, the media of communication do not help much. Understandably, the single chief executive is more "newsworthy" than the plural legislature. Dramatic events in Congress are the exception, not the rule, and coverage of the legislature is modest, even in the best media. So citizens who are attentive to legislative politics have a hard time comprehending fully what their representatives are up to in Washington.

Citizens who try to be attentive are relatively scarce. And those who form their own views and goals—the requirement of condition two—are even scarcer. The voting studies amply demonstrate that ballots are cast more on the basis of "party identification"—a voter's habitual commitment to one or the other of the major political parties—and the candidate's "image" than the issues of the day [Campbell et al. 1960, 1966].[13] While there is reason to believe that the 1950s were the nadir of issue orientation [RePass 1971; Boyd 1972; and Pomper 1972]—the "bland leading the bland"—it is doubtful that the upsurge in concern for issues and performance in the following decades was sufficient to satisfy the second accountability requirement. The voters' rejection of presidential candidates who sought to offer choices—Barry Goldwater in 1964 and George McGovern in 1972—seems to have reflected a general perception of the losers' "unsuitability" more than an awareness of their specific substantive views (although the former admittedly may flow from the latter). If this is true for presidential contests, it is most certainly true for less well-publicized legislative races. Again there is adequate basis for believing that vote choices in congressional elections seldom reflect detailed awareness of the candidates' issue positions.

The third condition for accountability, the opportunity for meaningful choice, is not well satisfied either. While in theory electoral contests provide voters with the opportunity to substitute candidates with whom they agree for incumbents whom they oppose, in practice the elections are limited in their effect because of two major factors. The relatively uninformed character of the voters is a major obstacle. If citizens know neither what the incumbent does in Washington nor what the major issues are in any campaign, they are unlikely to render an issue-related judgment at the polls, even when a clear, substantive choice exists between incumbent and challenger (and it does not in many districts). And the voters' preferred candidates may have no real chance to win. Most constituencies are "safe" for the incumbents or for their political party. In fact, there is little turnover in congressional seats; more than two-thirds of the House seats have stayed Republican or Democratic without change in recent years [Jones 1964]. Whatever change there is in Congress reflects what happens in about 100 or so highly competitive districts.[14]

In addition, change is not uniform. Variations in the nature of district electorates tend to cancel out the possibility that one set of views will gain ascendance in Congress. Voters in some districts may choose liberal challengers over conservative incumbents, but the reverse will occur in other constituencies. When the balance in the competitive districts tips in one direction, as it did to the

Democrats in 1964 and 1974, strong legislative majorities may come into existence. In the earlier period, with a Democrat in the White House, there was substantial policy change; in 1975–1976, with Gerald Ford as President, the Democratic two-thirds majority hardly proved "veto-proof."[15] Most commonly, the competitive districts do not swing uniformly to one party, and the overall composition of Congress will vary little from year to year. These modest changes in composition do not change the ideological outlook of the entire legislature.[16]

Accountability, then, works in imperfect ways. Elections are held every second year, at which time the voters can and sometimes do vote "no." But, in reality, they cast those ballots on the basis of little information about the incumbents' legislative performance, with scant concern for the issues that may separate the sitting legislators from their challengers, and in many districts with only a slight chance to send a new congressperson to Washington. Stability becomes the chief characteristic of the national legislature. Such change as occurs stems from electoral reversals in a small number of states and districts and is rarely sufficient to alter Congress' substantive outlook more than marginally.

SUMMARY

This assessment of the contemporary Congress—an institution decentralized in structure, which diffuses authority and requires a time-consuming process of negotiation and compromise to reach decisions—shows the legislature to be something less than ideal in terms of its responsiblity, responsiveness, and accountability. Congress simply is not equipped to be responsible on a regular basis; its organization and procedures are not designed to allow efficient and rapid formulation of policy. Congress has even delegated much of its policy-making power to the President, especially in international relations, and only the war in Indochina and the Watergate affair have provided much incentive for it to flex its muscles and try to recapture its atrophied authority. The legislature's performance is better in responsiveness. The same structural shortcomings that inhibit responsibility encourage representativeness. Many groups—but not all, and particularly not those interests lacking in money and skill—can find the time and the locus in the legislature to present their views prior to enactment of policy. Finally, Congress is held accountable in the sense that dissatisfied citizens can retire its members; in practice, these citizens lack the knowledge and/or the electoral opportunity to exercise meaningful popular control over public policy. Whatever the evaluative criteria employed, critics of all persuasions find Congress wanting. Each set, from its own particular vantage points, has specified reform proposals intended to make the legislature a "better" institution.

Notes

1. These topics are treated in detail in Rieselbach 1973. The positions enunciated are hardly radical. For verification of them the reader may wish to consult the leading texts in the field—Jewell and Patterson 1973, and Keefe and Ogul 1973.

2. The focus in this discussion will be on the 1971–1975 period. As will be noted, seemingly modest changes, such as the breach in 1971 of the seniority *principle*, may have highly significant results at a later time, such as the violation in 1975 of the seniority *practice*. It seems clear that Vietnam, Watergate, and their electoral consequences have contributed to some developments that may later alter the congressional process as described in this section.

3. The Committee on Rules defines, subject to the approval of the full House, the terms—the length of time for debate, the permissibility of amendments, and so on—under which the chamber considers a bill. The filibuster (or, technically, the cloture) rule in the Senate specifies the conditions under which debate can be terminated and a vote forced. For a full description of the rules and their strategic implications, see Froman 1967.

4. The Great Depression and the Hoover administration's inability to cope with it led voters to turn to Franklin Roosevelt and the Democrats in large numbers in the elections of 1932, 1934, and 1936. The singular combination of the assassination of John F. Kennedy and the 1964 Republican debacle, with Barry Goldwater at the top of the ticket, gave Democrats a genuine working majority in Congress for a brief period during the mid-1960s. The Democrats had a similar majority in the 94th Congress (1975–1976), but they were faced with a Republican President.

5. More often, however, the conflict has revolved around congressional efforts to impose its preferences—for public works, emergency housing, milk price support legislation—on an unwilling President. Richard Nixon vetoed 40 public bills, of which Congress overrode (by a two-thirds vote in each house) only 5. The legislature overrode 8 of Gerald Ford's first 43 vetoes.

6. In these sessions the committee goes over a bill line by line, often substantially amending it, in order to produce the final version of the legislation on which the full committee or the entire chamber will be asked to act.

7. On some occasions, a powerful individual can single-handedly block legislation. Chairman Wilbur D. Mills (D., Ark.) of the House Ways and Means Committee personally held off adoption of the principle of national health insurance for the elderly. Only when Mills became convinced of the need for such a program and steered an acceptable bill through his committee did Medicare become law.

8. The President, of course, does not personally make all these contacts and engage in all such negotiations. He has a large liaison staff, in his own White House Office and in the executive departments, at his disposal. The liaison organizations assist the President in persuading members of Congress to go along with his policy proposals; they serve as a chief communications device by which presidential-legislative accommodations are worked out. On liaison, see Holtzman 1970.

    The executive branch lobbying efforts may not always be supportive of the chief executive's programs, although they often seem to be. The agencies may ask Congress to depart from official executive requests because they do not feel satisfied with the authority or funds requested for them. Some bureaus—the Army Corps of Engineers, for instance—may develop such close ties with Congress that they become virtually immune from executive control.

9. For evidence suggesting that lobbyists have less "clout" then generally believed, that they are often understaffed and inadequately financed, and that they seek to avoid "pressure tactics" and the "hard sell," see Milbrath 1963, Dexter 1969, and Bauer et al. 1972.

10. This stress on the supportive rather than the aggressive posture of interest associations does not mean that other, more traditional techniques of influence are not used. Groups do hire intermediaries, influential constituents of the legislators, to express interest group sentiments. Some do get involved in the electoral process, seeking to reward their friends and punish their enemies. Others do engage in public relations campaigns intended to bring the weight of public opinion to bear on target legislators; occasionally, as recent convictions amply demonstrate, groups do resort to bribery. Yet, it seems clear that these tactics are relatively costly and inefficient. Direct communication is more effective and the preferred mode of group involvement.

11. The well-to-do, those with higher educations and incomes and with more leisure time, communicate more often than do low-income constituents and are an atypical sample.

12. This point should not be overemphasized. As noted, electoral uncertainties do compel congresspersons to worry about possible constituent reactions and thus

introduce some link between governor and governed. But this linkage is probably stronger than empirically necessary. Legislators need not worry about most single acts; rather they need to cultivate the impression among their constituents that they are alive, well, and, most important, working hard for the state or district.

13. One study found that in an off-year congressional election only 7 percent of those polled gave issue-related reasons for their votes. See Stokes and Miller 1962.

14. In 1972 in a typical congressional election only 13 incumbents were defeated, despite the Nixon landslide. Of the 69 freshmen in the House seated in January 1973, many were of the same party and point of view as the member whom they replaced. Two years later, in the first post-Watergate contests, an exceptionally large number of incumbents (40) lost their House seats; 92 newcomers, 75 of them Democrats, took office in January 1975. These two elections created a novel situation in that more than one-third of the House were either freshmen or beginning their second terms.

15. Reform did not become an issue after the former contest, but the latter gave additional impetus to a reform movement that had been gaining momentum since 1971.

16. A recent study finds that in the 1966 off-year House elections that selected the 90th Congress (1967–1968), losing candidates, as a group, bore a striking ideological similarity to the winners. That is, had the defeated nominees actually won, the resulting House would

have been slightly more liberal in foreign policy but slightly more conservative in the domestic sphere. To be sure, if the national electorate had followed party or liberal-conservative inclinations strongly in one direction, the resulting heavily Democratic or liberal (or Republican or conservative) Congress would have been far different from the 90th Congress actually elected. But such unidimensional swings in partisan or ideological preferences, encompassing virtually all electoral districts, are unknown in the annals of American politics. See Sullivan and O'Connor 1972. On the incumbent–challenger relationships see also Fishel 1973.

3.

Some Efforts at Reform, 1971-1975

WHAT CONSTITUTES A "BETTER" CONGRESS? EACH reformer proposes changes intended to move the legislature toward a particular vision of what Congress should be. Recent events have stimulated reform efforts, but Congress has moved in several directions rather than consistently toward any one reform vision. Reforms adopted in the first half of the seventies have sought improvements in responsibility, responsiveness, and accountability, but ironically the net impact of these often inconsistent changes may be to preserve the decentralized character of Congress.

Basically, two sets of changes have taken place. The first, a "democratizing" trend that further diffuses authority among a greater number of lawmakers, began with the passage of the 1970 Legislative Reorganization. The second, an effort to reassert congressional power and, thus, to enhance legislative responsibility, is the more immediate consequence of Vietnam and Watergate; it began in 1973 and gathered momentum after the Democratic sweep in the 1974 elections.

A DEMOCRATIZING TREND: RESPONSIVENESS AND ACCOUNTABILITY

The first reform thrust has been, in reality, a simultaneous shift toward responsiveness and accountability. More legislators representing more interests have been allowed to participate meaningfully in legislative affairs, and they have been required to act more openly and publicly.

Redistributing Committee Power

First the House and then the Senate began to loosen the hold of committee leaders on their panels. Seniority, followed strictly, guarantees that the majority party member with the longest continuous service on a committee becomes its chairman. But now seniority has lost its primacy. By 1971, both parties in the House decided they could employ criteria other than seniority to choose chairpersons; each empowered its party caucus, the meeting of all party members, to vote on whether to accept the recommendations of the party committee-on-committees for chairperson or ranking minority member.[1]

In 1973, the House Democrats went one step further: They determined that the full caucus should vote on the filling of each chair and, if one-fifth of the members so desired, by secret ballot. In practice, all decisions followed seniority, with negative votes against the senior committee member ranging from 2 to 49 and in no instance reaching one third of those cast. There were two challenges within the Republican conference in 1973, but the seniors retained their chairs by three-to-one margins. In that same year a hint of change reached the Senate when the Republicans adopted a proposal under which committee members would elect the ranking minority member from among their own number without regard to seniority; no deviations, in fact, occurred when the new process went into effect. In 1975, the Senate Democrats accepted a plan (which was not used to select chairpersons at the outset of the 94th Congress) to vote in full caucus by secret ballot for chairpersons upon the request of one-fifth of the caucus. In such balloting, members need not adhere to seniority.

It was the House Democrats who mounted the first successful challenge to seniority. In 1975, the caucus, its ranks enlarged by the addition of 75 freshmen, actually deposed of three elderly Southern committee chairmen:

W. R. Poage (Tex.), 75, of the Agriculture Committee; F. Edward Hébert (La.), 74, of the Armed Services Committee; and Wright Patman (Tex.), 81, of the Banking, Currency, and Housing panel. These aged oligarchs were succeeded by younger northerners: Thomas S. Foley (Wash.), 45; Melvin Price (Ill.), 70; and Henry S. Reuss (Wis.), 62. Foley and Price were the second-ranking Democrats on their committees while Reuss had stood fourth on the seniority ladder on the Banking Committee. A fourth chairman, Wayne Hays (Ohio) of the House Administration Committee, survived an initial negative caucus vote; Hays reportedly recaptured the support of numerous freshmen whose campaigns he had supported with funds at his disposal as chairman of the House Democratic Congressional Campaign Committee.[2] The upshot of these changes in the selection procedures in each chamber is likely to be far-reaching. Without the seniority rule's protection, House and Senate chairpersons will most certainly be more open to, and solicitous of, those who may vote to deprive them of their seats of power.

    The mode of choosing a chairperson is only important because this position commands considerable influence. If the committee leader were less powerful—more a presiding officer than an independent, autonomous force—conflict over seniority would be substantially reduced. The recent democratizing trend has in fact produced a number of reforms that limit the ability of chairpersons to dominate their panels. The 1970 Reorganization Act, for instance, provided that if a committee leader is absent from panel meetings, the committee may go about its business with the ranking majority member presiding. It also guaranteed all members the opportunity to participate fully in committee hearings (for example, by empowering minority members to call their own witnesses), limited the chair's ability to use proxy votes by mandating that they be given only in writing and for specific legislative business, and granted extra staff assistance to the minority members.

This 1970 act also sought to reduce the concentration of powerful Senate committee posts in a few hands. With appropriate protection for those already in office, it limited those elected subsequently to two major and one minor committee assignment and decreed that no senator may chair more than one committee or more than one subcommittee of a major panel. In 1971, the House Democrats also moved to reduce the concentration of power by barring committee leaders from heading more than one subcommittee on their panels; previously, chairpersons could assume the chair of any of their panel's subcommittees. In 1973 the House Democratic caucus secured subcommittee independence more fully by passing a so-called "subcommittee bill of rights." It mandated that while full committees would continue to define their subcommittees' jurisdictions, those jurisdictions, once defined, should be respected. Subcommittees were empowered to elect their own leaders, to write their own rules, and to have their own staffs. Each Democrat, in addition, was guaranteed a choice, following seniority, of one subcommittee membership, permitting each to seek a desired assignment [Ornstein 1975a]. In 1974, House Democrats, aiming mainly at the Appropriations Committee, decided to limit senior party members to service on a maximum of two of a committee's subcommittees. The impact of the new rule was to open up new places for junior representatives.

Control over staff has been diluted as well. Under the 1971 House reforms, no longer could the full-committee chairperson hire all panel staff. Each subcommittee leader, chair and ranking minority member, was granted the authority to hire a professional staff member for the committee. In 1975, the Senate went further, granting all senators some committee staff of their own. Previously, full- and subcommittee chairpersons had controlled the hiring of staff, but a new procedure permitted all senators not already authorized to employ staff personnel to recruit an aide to assist them with each (but not more than three) of their committee assignments. All in all, these changes reallocated committee power from senior leaders to rank-and-file members.

This democratizing impulse also led to a direct attack on two major House committees—Rules, and Ways and Means. The Rules Committee has had the power to determine the conditions under which legislation is considered on the House floor. A "closed" rule—to its critics, the "gag" rule—allowed the committee to limit or eliminate the opportunity to propose amendments to pending bills; thus, a majority may be unable to vote its will. To reduce this possibility, the Democrats adopted in 1973 a complicated procedure whereby if 50 party members propose and a majority of the full caucus agrees, the party delegation on Rules (almost always a majority of the panel in recent years) must agree to permit a floor vote on a particular amendment.[3] Ways and Means has also felt the lash of the democratizers. Under the chairmanship of Wilbur Mills (Ark.) the committee did not use subcommittees; all business was conducted in full committee with Mills presiding. In 1974, the Democrats adopted a resolution,[4] directed at Ways and Means, requiring all committees with more than 20 members have at least four subcommittees. Permanent, expert, and autonomous subcommittees were intended to undercut Mills' power; they have had the same effect on his successor, Al Ullman (Oreg.).

Taken together, these reforms have decentralized power in Congress even further. Committee chairpersons are less able to manage their panels; they must share their authority with subcommittee leaders and full committee majorities. The latter, with the demise of seniority, can oust the chairpersons. In other words, more people, operating from power bases within the committees and subcommittees, now have "a piece of the action," a share of congressional authority. Solutions to pressing policy problems will now require bargaining among a still larger set of legislators than has been customary; responsibility may be even harder to achieve. On the other hand, more lawmakers, speaking for differing sentiments and in contact with broader constituency interests, should bring more points of view into play in the course of legislative decision making. These democratizing reforms have extended congressional responsiveness.

Less Secrecy, More Accountability

A second set of developments has contributed, perhaps by inadvertence, to increased decentralization in Congress. These changes have promoted accountability by opening up congressional proceedings, but they have inhibited the growth of cohesive political parties, the most likely source of centralization and responsibility. The parties must compete for legislators' loyalty with the constituencies, interest groups, and ideological forces, among others. As Lewis Froman and Randall Ripley [1965] have suggested, parties will succeed more often when business is conducted out of the public eye. Partisan loyalty is generated more easily on procedural than on substantive questions, on issues of low rather than high public visibility. When matters are in the open, competing interests are likely to be aware of them, to mobilize their influence, and in consequence, to make it harder for a legislator to hew to the party line.

Over the past several years, critics of Congress have pointed to legislative secrecy as a major defect of the institution. Much of what goes on, including the critical decisions, seemed to take place in private, beyond public scrutiny. Recent revelations of members' conflicts of interest, ethical failings, and campaign finance abuses have contributed to pressures on Congress to revive its reputation for probity.

Recognizing the merit in these charges, the legislature has taken some steps to make its activities more accessible to interested citizens. Beginning in 1970, a series of moves has opened up committee proceedings. The Legislative Reorganization Act of that year allowed for televising, broadcasting, and photographing of committee hearings within limits left to the discretion of individual panels; so the provision makes possible but does not guarantee broad coverage of hearings. In 1973, the House mandated that all committee sessions be open, unless a majority of the panel voted to close them; this included the "mark-up" sessions in which final drafts of bills are prepared and which were often conducted behind closed doors. The Senate adopted similar rules in 1975. In both chambers, the burden of proof now falls on those who want to meet in secret; they must persuade their committee colleagues to keep the public out. Finally, in 1975, both chambers moved to open conference committee meetings, the sessions at which delegations from the two houses meet to reconcile differences in bills.[5] After March 1975, when the new rules were entirely in operation, more than 95 percent of all committee meetings were conducted in public.

The 1970 act also required that legislators vote publicly in committee and on the floor. Under the old rules, only total votes, not those of individual members, were recorded in committees. The revised procedures require the recording and publication of each lawmaker's votes in committee. Exposing committee voting makes it more difficult to take both sides of a question, one in the privacy of committee and another in public.

A related reform has shed light on congressional operations on the floor. Prior to the 1970 act, under certain circumstances no votes were recorded on the House floor: There could be voice, standing, or unrecorded teller votes,[6] but in each instance the positions of individual legislators remained unknown. Only roll call votes were recorded. The act provided that, on the demand of 20 House members, the names of those participating in teller votes be listed as they walk up the aisles. The effect of this reform has been to increase voting participation dramatically. Perhaps because their absence will be officially noted, many more members have turned up to vote; *Congressional Quarterly* [*Weekly Report*, March 4, 1972] estimates that in 1971 participation on teller votes increased "by more than 90%." Moreover, some liberals speculated that the new procedure helped them mobilize votes from those who might have contrived to be absent if teller votes were unrecorded [Ornstein and Rohde 1974]. In any case, recording votes, in committee and on the floor, has reduced the opportunity for lawmakers to hedge an issue by taking contradictory positions at different stages of the legislative process. It has also allowed attentive citizens to identify the supporters and opponents of particular legislative measures.

In the same vein, voters were often unable to determine whether members of Congress behaved as they did because of obligations to campaign contributors. Following the disclosures of manifold campaign finance abuses during the Watergate investigation, Congress enacted a sweeping reform bill in 1974. Individual and organizational contributors were severely limited—to $1000 and $5000, respectively—in what they could give to any primary, runoff, or general election campaign. Candidates were to campaign within spending ceilings. Both donors and recipients were obligated to report, fully and promptly, even modest campaign contributions.[7]

The constitutionality of this bill was challenged, and

in January 1976 the Court struck down the provision for spending ceilings on the basis that it violated First Amendment guarantees of freedom of expression. Still, the decision did sustain both the contribution limits and the reporting requirements of the act. Thus, while candidates may spend unlimited funds, they must raise the money from relatively small contributions and report how they spend their funds. If effective, and the law provides for enforcement, these latter requirements should let the public know where candidates' funds come from and how they are spent. Such "sunshine" operations may, in addition, help remove popular doubts about legislators' pursuit of their own interests at the expense of the public's.

Overall, these reforms run counter to increased congressional centralization; they foster responsiveness and accountability at the expense of responsibility. Because more lawmakers now share in legislative power, more opinions may have to be taken into account prior to policy decisions. More public attention now focuses on representatives and senators; in consequence, they may need to respond more to popular, and less to party, pressures. To the extent that more points of view are heard during the course of congressional deliberations, the legislature is likely to become a more responsive institution.

One caveat is essential here. These democratizing reforms may make the House and Senate, and their committees and subcommittees, more open and responsive but when conditions are right, the legislature may be responsive only to presidential or partisan interests. That is, if the majorities that have been freed to assume control of committees and floor proceedings are large and cohesive enough or are dedicated presidential loyalists, they may monopolize the levers of legislative authority. Such a powerful majority might be able to overcome the decentralization—and the increased reliance on a bargaining style of decision making that flows from it—that these recent reforms are expected to produce. Something of this sort was predicted for the 94th Congress (1975-1976) with its lopsided Democratic majority, but it did not develop as that majority, despite its numbers, turned out to be considerably less cohesive than expected.

A TREND TOWARD RESPONSIBILITY

The second trend of the early 1970s, flowing directly from congressional reaction to Vietnam and Watergate and aided by the Democratic sweep in the 1974 legislative elections, has been toward increased congressional responsibility. There has been both an institutional effort to restore Congress' authority vis-à-vis the executive branch and an attempt by an unusually large Democratic majority to control the legislative apparatus to enact a liberal program. In the 1973-1976 period, this centralizing thrust has intersected with the democratizing trend, clouding Congress' future considerably.

Specifically, Congress has moved to reassert its prerogatives in the foreign policy sphere. This has long been a congressional concern. In 1954 reformers in the Senate came within a single vote of passing the Bricker Amendment to the Constitution. This proposal would have limited presidential discretion in foreign affairs by curbing the practice of conducting diplomacy through executive agreements, as opposed to treaties. The Senate has the power to give advice and consent only to commitments embodied in treaty form.[8]

These efforts, following a somewhat different tack, reached fruition in 1973. Frustrated by a general inability to influence the conduct of the war in Indochina in more than marginal ways and emboldened by the Nixon Administration's Watergate embarrassments, Congress passed, over a presidential veto, a War Powers bill, limiting to 60 days the chief executive's authority to commit military forces to combat without explicit congressional approval. Such legislation reestablishes Congress as a force to reckon with in military affairs, although it is not at all certain that the legislature would seek to cancel military action that a President asserted was in the "national interest." Beyond war powers legislation Congress has made a concerted effort, of uncertain long-range impact, to influence the shape of national policy toward such countries as Vietnam, Cambodia, Panama, Turkey, and Angola.

Budgetary reform is another area in which Congress has reasserted its authority and increased its capacity to influence policy. Impartial observers as well as critics have long agreed that Congress has failed to exercise its power of the purse effectively. As a result, the President has justified impounding (refusing to spend) appropriated funds as necessary to sustain fiscal responsibility. The chief executive submits a single unified budget, but Congress, through its Appropriations Committees, used to split the program into a dozen or more bills that were given separate, unrelated treatment. At no point did the interested lawmaker have occasion to see how the total budget looked and to compare total proposed expenditures with available revenue.[9] Rather, the full picture was not visible until all appropriations measures had been passed; thus the last bills in the series became major targets for reduction as the sums committed in the earlier bills began to mount. What was cut at one point could, of course, be restored later, in supplemental appropriations bills, a fact that probably encouraged legislators to make cuts for partisan reasons in the full knowledge that such reductions need not be permanent. What was needed to remedy these defects—to reduce Congress' competitive disadvantage in the face of executive experts and to give the legislature the opportunity to set its own spending priorities—was to coordinate and centralize to some degree the congressional consideration of the budget.

Congress has made the effort. Building on the recommendations of a Joint Study Committee on Budget Control, created in 1972, the legislature passed two years later a comprehensive Budget and Impoundment Control Act. *1974* The bill created special budget committees in the House and Senate that draw on the resources of a Congressional Budget Office (CBO), a unified, joint staff of skilled experts. By April 15 of every year, each budget committee is to report a first budget resolution setting a tentative ceiling on federal spending and specifying the maximum that can be spent within various subareas of the budget. On or before May 15, the two chambers must agree on and pass the resolution, which also specifies federal revenues, the deficit (or surplus) for the fiscal year, and the amount of the public debt. Only after that date can the Appropriations Committees report regular appropriations bills; these panels are limited by the ceilings contained in the resolution. By September 15, two weeks before the start of the fiscal year, Congress must adopt a second, and binding, budget resolution that commits the legislature to firm figures for outlays, revenues, and the deficit. Thereafter neither house can consider legislation that increases expenditures or reduces revenues beyond the amounts in the second resolution. As the fiscal year progresses, a reconciling resolution can be passed, if needed, to cover any altered circumstances that may develop. A tax surcharge can be considered at the end of the fiscal year to make up any additional deficit that may occur.

Although not required by the 1974 act, Congress attempted an incomplete trial run during 1975. The budget committees, handicapped because the CBO was not in full operation, chose not to try to set expenditure ceilings in the subareas of the budget. They did, however, include "target" figures in their reports on the second resolution.

The results of these first efforts at implementation are mixed, but, on the whole, promising. The first resolution passed the House by only four votes, opposed by liberals who felt spending was too low and conservatives who believed the deficit was too large. The second resolution was passed nearly two months late, reflecting in large part legislative difficulty in allocating the administration's proposals, presented in 16 functional categories, among the 15 appropriations bills with which Congress handles the budget.

Despite these problems, the fiscal 1976 budget did reflect congressional priorities to a considerable extent. The lawmakers raised spending $25 billion above administration estimates; the deficit was $5.6 billion over executive projections. More importantly, appropriations in particular categories differed markedly from the executive's proposals: Cuts were inflicted on defense and foreign aid outlays; more was allocated for education and social welfare programs. In addition, the process contributed to financial restraint. The Senate, for instance, rejected the conference report on the 1976 Military Procurement Bill and sustained President Ford's veto of legislation raising milk price supports when its Budget Committee forcefully pointed out that these measures would "bust the budget."

If the remaining difficulties are overcome and the new process works effectively when fully implemented, the budget procedure should enable Congress to match the executive branch's Office of Management and Budget in expertise and, thus, to set its spending priorities with confidence. The President may, of course, disagree with congressional allocations, and conflict will surely follow, but the struggle will be fought on terrain more favorable to Congress than has been the case in recent years.

The Budget Act also curbs the executive practice of impounding funds Congress has authorized and appropriated. If the President wishes to defer spending, either house can compel expenditure of the funds by passing a resolution to that effect. If the chief executive seeks to terminate programs or reduce total spending, he must persuade both houses to rescind the appropriation within 45 days; if the chambers do not act, he must spend the funds.[10] Under the new law Congress has been able to assert its spending priorities and to diminish the power of the chief executive to spend selectively. This is in sharp contrast to the Nixon years. The legislature has, to date, rejected more than 90 percent of the proposed deferrals and rescissions. To do so, however, has required the lawmakers and their staffs to take on additional paperwork, much of it dealing with trivial matters and relatively small and noncontroversial amounts.

Finally, on the institutional level, Congress has moved to strengthen its information resources. In 1972, it established an Office of Technological Assessment, which has supplied analysis of the potential impact of various scientific programs that have been enacted and proposed by Congress. Also, throughout the early 1970s the legislature has provided more staff assistance for its members and its committees. If useful data flow from such innovations, the legislature may be better able to develop and sustain its own policy initiatives. In sum, these developments—more authority and more information—may contribute to Congress' ability to compete effectively with the executive.

The impetus for legislative responsibility has come largely from liberal Democrats in the House, who have sought, especially in the 94th Congress, to convert the party caucus into a disciplined force for the support of progressive legislation. The liberals scored a triumph, more symbolic than meaningful, in securing the abolition of the House Internal Security (formerly, Un-American Activities) Committee, long a target of liberal criticism. Much more importantly, they brought about a strengthening of the party apparatus. Extending some modest changes made in 1973, the caucus in 1975 established a new procedure for making party committee assignments. In 1973, the party leaders—the Speaker, the Floor Leader, and the Whip—were permitted to sit with the Ways and Means Democrats, who had traditionally served as the party's Committee-on-Committees, to make committee assignments. At the same time, the Democrats established a Steering and Policy Committee, a 24-member body composed of the party's elected leaders (the Speaker, Floor Leader, and Caucus Chairperson), 12 members elected by the caucus to represent geographic regions, and 9 others appointed by the Speaker (including the party whips and representatives of the black caucus, women members, and freshmen Democrats). In 1975, in the 94th Congress, the caucus dramatically stripped the Ways and Means contingent of its committee-on-committees powers, transferring them to the Steering and Policy Committee. The shift put the party's committee assignments into the hands of a more liberal body.[11] The caucus, of course, retained the right to vote on each nomination for a committee chair.

The impact of the strengthened caucus can be seen in the liberalization of Ways and Means. Long a bastion of fiscal conservatism under Wilbur Mills' chairmanship, that body became a symbol and a challenge for reform-minded Democrats. As noted, the resolution to create at least four subcommittees was an obvious effort to dilute the chairperson's power. In addition, the caucus voted to enlarge the size of Ways and Means from 25 to 37 members. This meant that 12 new members could be appointed to sit with 13 holdovers on the Democratic side of the committee table. The Steering and Policy Committee awarded eight of these vacancies to representatives who had served in the 93rd Congress. A comparison of their voting records with those of the 13 returning members makes clear the changed cast of the committee. The new appointees averaged 11.1 percent lower support for the conservative coalition and 10.3 percent greater party unity than the carryover members of Ways and Means.[12]

In 1975, however, the more liberal committee—operating with a new chairman, with six subcommittees, and in open sessions—lost, temporarily at least, much of the cohesiveness and power that it had possessed previously. On several occasions, the liberal members insisted, over their chairman's objections, on taking amendments rejected in committee to the House floor. On some of these they won, thus undercutting the committee's prestige in the process. In addition, Ways and Means suffered a crushing defeat when its energy tax bill was rewritten on the floor. In sum, the caucus' efforts to control the committee ran afoul of the democratizing aspects of congressional reform, producing "more confusion but few legislative results during a tempestuous year" [*Congressional Quarterly Weekly Report*, January 10, 1976, p. 40].

In the 94th Congress the party caucus took on other powers intended to promote liberal causes. The Democrats empowered the Speaker to fill vacancies on the powerful Rules Committee; Carl Albert's choice of two committed liberals (John Moakley of Massachusetts and Andrew Young of Georgia) virtually ensured that the panel would give strong support to the party leadership. The caucus also extended the principle of elective chairpersons by assuming the authority to vote on the nominations of all chairpersons of Appropriations subcommittees. In fact, the senior Democrat was nominated and ratified in each case, but the incumbent subcommittee leaders, who have considerable authority in fiscal decisions, are now on notice that they need the support of their caucus colleagues. The caucus declined to make the post of party Whip elective; perhaps to avoid a direct reproach to their leaders or to recognize the competent performance of the incumbent, the Democrats left the selection of the Whip to their Floor Leader. The caucus retains the power to bind its members, by a two-thirds vote, to support its decisions about the election of House leaders and committee chairpersons and to instruct committees to report legislation. But in 1975, perhaps in the spirit of democratization, it yielded its seldom-used authority to commit the members' roll call votes.

In March 1975, the Senate, after weeks of acrimonious debate and complex parliamentary maneuvering, made a somewhat significant rules change. The upper chamber voted to modify its (in)famous cloture rule, making it a little easier to cut off debate and end filibusters. Previously, two-thirds of those present and voting (or 67, if all 100 senators were in attendance) were required to invoke cloture; under the new rule three-fifths of the full membership (60 votes) can bring debate to an end. The change was in fact a compromise; liberals had wanted to enable a simple majority of those present and voting to force a conclusion to a filibuster.[13]

The real impact of this reform remains unclear. There were 103 cloture votes between 1917 and 1975 under the two-thirds rule. Twenty-four were successful, including two that concluded debate on the change in filibuster rule; 16 of these occurred during the 1971–1975 period, indicating a marked decline in minority power in recent years. The filibuster has claimed only one bill (a 1974 proposal to establish a consumer protection agency) that would have passed under a three-fifths rule. In four other cases, 60 votes were cast for cloture, but the two-thirds needed to end debate were subsequently attained and the measures passed. On the other hand, under a simple majority principle, 24 additional cloture votes would have succeeded. In 1975, the Senate passed two measures after ending debate by more than 60 but fewer than two-thirds of the votes cast, but neither became law. One, an antibusing amendment against which liberals conducted a filibuster was dropped in conference. The second, the common-site picketing bill opposed by conservatives, did not have sufficient support to survive a presidential veto. As these examples suggest, the reform may have only marginal effect, but it is most certainly a move toward reducing the ability of a Senate minority to prevent a majority from acting. Whatever effect the change has will be in the direction of enhancing senatorial responsibility.

In general, the push for responsibility made genuine progress during the 1973-1975 period. Armed with greater information and enlarged authority, Congress is certainly better situated to advance serious alternatives to the President's legislative program. In the 94th Congress, liberal domination, especially in the House Democratic caucus, may indeed clear the way for a burst of progressive legislation. Even so, this push toward responsibility may be more illusory than real. It remains uncertain that Congress will use its newly won foreign policy powers with any real effect, or that it will implement and follow through on its revised budget procedures to gain a new voice in fiscal affairs. Finally, there is little chance that liberals can retain for long the top-heavy majorities they possessed during 1975-1976. When the electoral tide recedes and a more normal liberal-conservative distribution of congressional seats recurs, it may be considerably more difficult to sustain a progressive policy impulse.

The democratizing and liberalizing trends of the early 1970s happened to converge in the 94th Congress. At the same time that there are more positions of power from which more lawmakers operate more openly, liberals have secured command of most of the levers of authority.[14] (At least this has been true in the House; the situation has been more fluid in the Senate.) In other words, there has been simultaneous movement toward responsiveness and accountability (through diffusion of authority and less secrecy in congressional operations) and toward responsibility (through assumption of foreign policy and fiscal powers and strengthened party apparatus). This situation is clearly unstable in the long run. Liberal Democratic strength, which is exceptionally high during the 1975–1976 period, seems certain to diminish. But it is reasonable to speculate, especially in view of the Ways and Means experience, that the move toward responsiveness (decentralization) is likely to survive and endure. If so, the prognosis is for the survival of the bargaining, compromising, negotiation style of decision making that has long characterized Congress.[15] The essential questions remain: Can a decentralized legislature do the job? If not, what enduring reforms are in order?

Notes

1. The Republican procedure called for a conference vote on the committee-on-committees' recommendation, a suggestion that need not follow the seniority principle. The Democrats adopted a plan, sometimes called a "Kamikaze system," whereby ten committee members could force a vote in caucus on their chairperson. The requirement to stand up publicly to oppose powerful chairpersons served to deter challengers, but there was one challenge in the Democratic caucus. Liberals on the District of Columbia Committee sought to oust chairman John L. McMillan (S.C.), objecting to his long opposition to home rule for Washington, D.C., but lost on a 126–96 caucus vote. Whether this substantial challenge contributed to McMillan's defeat in his district's 1972 primary is a moot point.

2. One additional change in committee leaders occurred in the House in 1975. After a series of widely publicized escapades with an exotic dancer, Wilbur Mills, (Ark.), 63, long reputed to be one of the most powerful men in the House, declined to seek reelection as chairman of the Ways and Means Committee. He was replaced by Al Ullman (Oreg.), 60, the second-ranking Democrat on the committee. Subsequently Mills publicly acknowledged that he suffered from alcoholism and began a lengthy period of treatment and convalescence. Mills eventually returned to work, but in early 1976 he announced that he would retire from Congress at the conclusion of the 94th Congress. Incidentally, Representatives Patman and Hébert, two other deposed chairmen, also retired, effective in January 1977.

3. In February 1975, this procedure was used to permit the first House vote on whether to retain the contro-

versial oil depletion allowance. This tax benefit for oil
producers was designed to stimulate exploration for
new petroleum sources but was denounced as a tax
loophole by its critics. The Democratic caucus voted
153–98 to instruct the party's Rules Committee delegation to permit a vote on an amendment (to a major
tax reduction bill) to repeal the allowance. The members of Rules complied with the instruction and the
full House voted to eliminate the allowance.

4. The reform spirit in the House led to the establishment
    of a Select Committee on Committees with Richard
    Bolling (D., Mo.) as chairman. When this panel pro-
    duced a sweeping set of reform proposals, far too
    "radical" to be widely acceptable (see U.S. Congress
    1974), a Democratic caucus group, chaired by Julia
    Butler Hansen (Wash.), produced a more modest and
    less consequential set of reforms, including the re-
    quirement for Ways and Means subcommittees, which
    was eventually passed.

5. Moreover, the House Democrats decided in 1975 to
    open their party caucus. They mandated that the
    caucus agenda be available five days before the meet-
    ing; that discussions of legislation be open to the pub-
    lic unless a majority, voting in public, chooses to close
    the meeting; and that the caucus proceedings be pub-
    lished. While discussions of caucus rules changes, of
    committee assignments, and of election of House and
    committee leaders remain closed and off-the-record,
    the changes adopted make party deliberations more
    accessible to the interested citizen.

6. Under House rules a device known as the Committee
    of the Whole House on the State of the Union is used to
    facilitate preliminary consideration of legislation.

The Speaker need not preside; a quorum is 100, not the 218 required when the House sits formally. Voting in this committee is by voice vote; standing vote, whereby the presiding officer counts the "yeas" and then the "nays" as each group in turn rises; or teller vote, whereby each group (yea and nay) comes forward in the chamber to be counted as they pass between tellers. When the Committee of the Whole concludes preliminary consideration, it "rises," the Speaker resumes the chair, and a quorum reverts to 218. The House then acts to review—ratify or reject—decisions taken in the Committee of the Whole.

7. For a full description of the 1974 Act, see *Congressional Quarterly Weekly Report*, October 12, 1974, pp. 2865–2870; on the Supreme Court decision, consult the *Congressional Quarterly Weekly Report*, February 7, 1976, pp. 267–274.

8. Reformers also have reservations about broad delegations of authority for executive control of foreign trade policy; they hold that Congress should determine tariff levels on its own initiative.

9. Such calculations about the relationship between revenues and expenditures are very difficult and complex. For one thing, agencies, especially in the Defense Department, with the approval of the appropriate committee, subcommittee, or ranking member thereof, can "re-program" funds; that is, they can spend them on activities other than those for which they were originally appropriated. For another, money is often "in the pipeline"—appropriated but unspent—and a cut in subsequent appropriations will not affect programs until unspent funds are exhausted. Finally, agencies may spend via

"backdoor" spending—through borrowing, permanent appropriations, or mandatory spending—which is beyond the legislature's annual appropriations power. For a useful summary of the problems of conventional budgetary practice, see *Congressional Quarterly Weekly Report*, April 28, 1973, pp. 1013–1018.

10. Note that these anti-impoundment provisions tip the balance of power in the legislature's direction: Either house can require spending of appropriated funds, but both must agree to rescinding enacted appropriations.

11. *Congressional Quarterly* data make this clear: In the 93rd Congress, the 15 Ways and Means Democrats averaged 34.1 percent in support of the southern Democratic-Republican conservative coalition; in that same Congress, the 22 Democrats who were subsequently appointed to the Steering Committee in the 94th Congress (Speaker Carl Albert and freshman Representative William Brodhead did not vote in the 93rd) averaged only 24.9 percent in support of the conservative coalition, a difference of 9.2 percent. Similarly, in the 93rd Congress, Ways and Means Democrats averaged 61.3 percent on party unity while the 22 voting members of the 1975 Steering Committee supported the party majority 74.9 percent of the time, a difference of 13.6 percent. In short, the Steering Committee, now empowered to make committee assignments subject to caucus ratification, is decidedly less conservative and more inclined than the Ways and Means Democrats to support partisan majorities.

12. In addition, two of the four new appointees to Ways and Means who had *not* served in the 93rd Congress

(Andy Jacobs of Indiana and Abner Mikva of Illinois) were former members who had established solid liberal records. Al Ullman's accession to the committee chairmanship, following Wilbur Mills' forced resignation, made only a slight difference; the liberals had enhanced their position substantially before the change in chairmen.

13. At the center of the reform issue was the question of whether the Senate can adopt new rules by simple majority vote at the start of each Congress. Despite Vice-President Nelson Rockefeller's affirmative ruling on this question, the defenders of the filibuster, led by Senator James B. Allen (D., Ala.), outmaneuvered the reformers and salvaged the compromise, which not only imposed the 60-vote, rather than a simple majority, rule, but also reversed Rockefeller's ruling and established that a two-thirds vote is still required to end debate on changes in Senate rules.

14. The intersection of these trends is clearly visible in the ouster of the House chairmen, noted above. Representatives Poage and Hébert, in particular, were both autocratic in their control of their committees and conservative in their policy preferences. Thus the democratizers and the liberals joined forces to remove them, and to breach the seniority rule as well.

15. Of course, many of the reforms of 1971–1975 will probably survive any alterations in political circumstances. What does seem certain is that a recognizable form of decentralized legislature will continue to exist, precipitating more discussion of the reform issues posed here.

4.

The Future Congress: Some Alternative Visions

WHATEVER THE OUTCOME OF THE CONTEMPORARY reform movements, some observers of Congress are certain to remain unsatisfied and to continue to propose reforms.[1] Depending on whether values of responsibility, responsiveness, accountability, or some combination of these criteria motivate them, their suggestions tend to fall into identifiable categories. The important point is that reforms designed to promote one value may have costs in another. Here we will note some major reformist visions and assess their potential impact on the evaluative criteria under consideration.

A RESPONSIBLE CONGRESS

There are two quite separate and distinct perspectives on the appropriate way in which to achieve congressional responsibility—one subordinates the legislature to the executive and the other envisions congressional supremacy—but both desire to centralize legislative operations. Each vision points to the fragmentation of power created by multiple centers of decision-making authority as the vice that prevents Congress from efficiently formulating public policy. Each seeks to bring some order out of congressional chaos; each wants to make it easier for Congress to act promptly and effectively. Each proposes reforms that, as we shall see, reduce political responsiveness.[2]

The pro-presidential point of view, in the past a proposal favored by liberals, suggests that the gradual emergence of the President as chief policy maker and administrator is both inevitable and desirable. Congress, in this scheme of things, would devote its energies to nonpolicy activities, such as overseeing the executive branch—to ensure that the agencies and bureaus conduct their affairs in keeping with policy goals—and acting as a "service" agency for citizens—to provide the populace with a point of contact with government. In short, Congress would concede lawmaking to the President, occasionally modifying proposals from that office but largely legitimatizing them. Legislative attention would be directed to policing the bureaucracy and serving the citizenry.

Frequently, and especially among academics, the "executive-dominance" notion is incorporated in a broader political (and constitutional) reform movement, the "responsible two-party system."[3] This scheme seeks to centralize the policy-making process through the agency of the disciplined political party. The British parliamentary arrangements provide a model of the sort of order that these reformers envision.[4] As leader, the President, like the Prime Minister, would have the ability to win approval for favored programs and to control their implementation. Support from Congress would be virtually assured, for the legislators, given their dependence in the new order on powerful political parties, could oppose the executive only upon pain of terminating their political careers. Popular accountability, not an independent legislature, is the control mechanism; the electorate would punish poor performance by voting the party responsible out of office. In this view, then, Congress would yield its lawmaking authority, becoming instead a part of the party "team," concentrating on oversight and public service activities.

Strengthening the presidency, regardless of whether it is part of an invigorated party system, would entail alterations both in the system of electing legislators and in the internal operations of Congress. On the electoral front, the reformer's intent is to undercut the independence of the contemporary legislator. This might be accomplished by the oft-proposed, never seriously considered extension of lawmakers' terms of office, to four years in the House and eight years in the Senate. All members of Congress, then, would be selected simultaneously with the President. Presumably they would sense their obligation to him, insofar as they understood that they owed their electoral success to his efforts more than to their own.

Lengthening congressional terms might encourage loyalty to the White House but it would in no way compel it, especially if the election produced a President of one party and a legislative majority of the other. Thus, the party-responsibility reformers desire to guarantee party government, and in consequence, presidential government. They would have new, centralized national party committees control the fate of the party's congressional candidates; the powerful party organizations would control campaign finance and would manage a national campaign on national issues. If the ultimate power to control the nomination—to exact loyalty pledges in advance or to deprive recalcitrant legislators of their seats—rested with the President and his national committee, then he, like the British Prime Minister, could count on a reliable legislative majority in support of his program.

The pro-presidential reformers also propose numerous alterations in congressional operations, all intended to reduce the ability of various minorities to block the President's program. Most importantly, these suggestions seek ways to curb the independence and autonomy that currently characterizes the operation of congressional committees. These reformers approve of the 1971–1975 changes that reduce the powers of the panel chairpersons, enabling a majority of committee members to control their behavior. If the President could, under such circumstances, command a panel majority, he would be able to move his proposals through the committees. A more basic way of gaining control of the committees would be to ensure that the chairpersons, especially if they continued to wield substantial authority, were party loyalists. The abandonment of the seniority rule in 1975 may well make it possible for majorities in Congress to select cooperative colleagues as committee leaders.

Both modes of curtailing committee autonomy—replacing seniority with an elective process and reducing the powers of the committee leaders—correspondingly elevate the legislative parties to prominent positions, and the executive-dominance reformers applaud these changes. Party leaders, they insist, should assume the role of presidential representatives on Capitol Hill rather than acting as legislative emissaries to the White House, as is current practice. The leaders should commit themselves and the resources at their disposal to advancing the President's program.

Party agencies should pursue the same end. The caucus should be able to exercise power on behalf of the majority of its partisans; it should control committee assignments, for example, rewarding the faithful and punishing the disloyal. Policy committees should set forth party positions, subject to review and ratification by the full party membership, and at the operating level should be empowered to schedule party-sponsored bills for prompt floor consideration. In the House, as noted, there has been movement in this direction. If linked to responsible parties able to punish dissenters through control of the nominating process, such changes would create powerful parties capable of steering executive programs through the legislature.

The reformers seeking to smooth the congressional path of executive policies would change the rules of procedure as well. Here, too, the goal is to reduce the ability of minorities, entrenched at particular veto points within a decentralized system, to block administration programs. In the House, the chief focus of reform is the Rules Committee. One suggestion, recently adopted, is to place party loyalists on the committee. Another is to reinstitute and make permanent the 21-day rule, under which the Speaker can, over committee objections, call up measures for floor consideration after the bill has been in the Rules Committee's hands for more than 21 days. On the two occasions that it has been adopted, most recently during the 89th Congress (1965–1966), the provision has facilitated the movement of legislation to the floor, but in each instance it did not survive renewed conservative strength and was stricken from the rules. Another proposal, applicable to all committees, would alter the discharge rule: The number of legislators' signatures required to extract a bill from an unwilling committee would be reduced from the present 218, a majority of the full chamber, to some more readily attainable number, such as 150. Such changes would limit the ability of the committees to block passage of measures favored by a majority, including a presidential majority, in the full chamber.

On the Senate side, the reformers' main target has been the obvious one—unlimited debate. Their suggestions to control debate include eliminating various delaying tactics and distracting procedures,[5] leaving more time to deal with substantive legislation; limiting the amount of time any senator can hold the floor; requiring that debate be relevant to the issue at hand; and reducing the opportunity to mount a filibuster.[6] As noted, they have succeeded to a certain extent in their most important objective: altering the cloture rule to allow a smaller majority (60 senators) to terminate debate. Each of these changes should curtail a minority's potential to tie up the Senate in the interest of defeating specific bills.

A potential presidential weapon is often discussed in this context: the item veto. At the present time, the chief executive must accept or reject a bill *in toto*, but with an item veto he could block enactment of single provisions without having to reject an entire bill. Such a move would eliminate one legislative strategy for asserting congressional policy-making initiatives: the inclusion of a few items opposed by the chief executive in legislation containing major programs he favors. It is assumed that the President will accept a few undesirable provisions rather than risk losing a matter of central concern.[7] Executive impoundment was employed, especially by the Nixon administration, as a partial, and perhaps unconstitutional, substitute for the item veto. But the new Budget Act enables Congress to limit drastically the executive's ability to impound funds without legislative concurrence.

All these suggestions, whether adopted wholly or in part, singly or in combination, would basically alter the position of Congress in the national political process: Fragmentation of power would be diminished, centralization increased, committee independence restricted, the parties strengthened, and the rules altered—all to permit executive leadership to carry the day. In the responsible party vision, the executive would dominate his national party and, through it, the legislature. By controlling campaign finance, the parties would control congressional nominations and the legislative careers of the electoral winners. The presidential candidate of each party would run on a clearly defined party platform, and the voters would select the program that best suited them. The victor would have a dependable legislative majority to enact his policies; the centralized, party-managed Congress would do his bidding.

This scenario can be described as a responsibility-accountability vision. Such arrangements would be responsible because effective solutions to pressing problems could be efficiently and promptly produced. They would be subject to accountability because the voters would retain the ability to replace a governing party with an opposition that persuaded the electorate it could do more and do it better.[8] The cost of all this, of course, is in responsiveness. With Congress subordinate to executive-dominated political parties, the channels of communication now used by many groups to present their views to a legislature able to implement those ideas would disappear or become mere formalities. Congress would not be able to respond to citizen and group sentiments or translate them into policy. These views would have to focus on the President. While he would no doubt have to calculate what public reaction to his initiatives might do to his party's fortunes, he nevertheless would have broad authority to chart the country's course for four years (or six, if Nixon's proposal for a single, six-year presidential term should find a receptive audience). In any event, the executive-dominace school would stress responsibility at the expense of responsiveness.

There is another, less widely discussed, vision that focuses, to some extent at least, on responsibility. This view, the congressional-supremacy position, is the mirror image of the executive-dominance orientation, but it seeks to establish Congress as the dominant force in national politics. This line of argument, often labeled the "literary" or "whig" theory, holds that the legislature ought to exercise all powers in all areas. The President, by contrast, would have considerably less initiative and would commit himself more to the execution of congressionally determined policies [Burnham 1959; de Grazia 1965].

To establish this congressional-supremacy vision would, obviously, require many reforms. One would be to centralize legislative operations, in ways not unlike those that the pro-executive forces propose but with the power relation with the White House reversed, so that Congress would call the shots rather than respond to presidential leadership. But the President, building on his constitutional commander-in-chief power as well as on considerable precedent, has become too strong for serious challenge. The federal government has become too large and too involved in too many areas to be stripped of all its authority and responsibility. Burnham [1959] proposes, in effect, to dismantle the federal apparatus and turn most of its present duties over to the state and local governments. Most observers, however, discount this idea as unrealistic. The Nixon admininstration's various revenue-sharing proposals—a short step toward a reallocation of authority, if not of funding sources, within the federal system—have found only modest support even among those who are the direct recipients of the money.

Few critics of the executive-dominance scheme have gone so far as to suggest that legislative dominance is desirable or even workable. Even members of Congress, understandably unsympathetic to subordinating the legislature to any branch, do not seek to master the executive. Rather those who look to a resurgent Congress seek to redress the balance, to stem the historical flow of authority to the President, and to reassert the need for congressional perspectives to be heard and to prevail when sufficiently supported by the people. In short, these critics of executive force envision governmental decision making that is responsive to the sorts of interests only Congress is capable of representing adequately.

A RESPONSIVE CONGRESS

The pro-legislative reformers, essentially, do not seek to subordinate the executive, but they do value both responsiveness and congressional power. Their intent is to make legislative participation in policy formation meaningful, and to allow Congress to assert its own priorities, even over executive opposition, without resort to excessive centralization. Their ideas, including those implemented in the 1971–1975 period, lead to even more diffusion of authority and to intensified bargaining as the dominant means of conflict resolution.[9]

Promotion of congressional responsiveness and power entails particular views on electoral politics and congressional structures and procedures. The pro-congressional forces stand firm against reapportionment and any effort to impose national, disciplined political parties. Indeed, the very "localism," the concern for local as opposed to national interests, deplored by believers in executive dominance, is a positive virtue for those who back legislative power. Reapportionment, even to reflect simple population equality, and subscription to a national party platform, compelled by the ability of the national party to inflict electoral defeat, would work to minimize the representation of diverse interests, especially those geographically dispersed or otherwise incapable of representation through population alone.[10] Thus, an election system like the one we now have, in which candidates remain free to build their own organizations, raise their own funds, take their own issue positions, and appeal to whatever groups they deem appropriate, is desirable; this system allows the widest possible array of differing viewpoints to find expression in Congress.

As for the internal operations of Congress, those favoring responsiveness have resisted efforts to reduce committee autonomy, to impose centralization by strengthening political parties, or to foster both objectives through changes in the rules. Thus, they opposed alteration of the seniority system and of the basic powers of committee leaders. But even though election of committee chairpersons could permit a disciplined majority to gain control of the panels, such a result seems unlikely unless selection of the chair is linked to a general centralization of legislative authority.[11] Therefore, under current conditions, modification of the seniority principle seems most likely to diffuse power further, to give panel majorities the ability to replace or control reluctant chairpersons, and, thus, to enhance responsiveness.

Recent changes in the committee assignment process also seem to spread rather than concentrate influence in Congress. For some years, the so-called "Johnson Rule," initiated during Lyndon B. Johnson's tenure as Majority Leader, has guaranteed each senator one major committee post before any colleague can receive a second choice assignment. The 1973 and 1975 changes, especially the protection of House subcommittee independence, go far toward providing every member with a place on a committee or subcommittee with jurisdiction over important legislative business. At the same time, however, the transfer of House Democratic committee assignment power to the Steering and Policy Committee may, but need not, constitute a move toward centralization; it is unlikely that the leaders will seek to dominate the assignment process totally.[12] In short, the committee assignment process at present seems to contribute to diffusion of legislative authority and, thus, to the Congress' responsiveness.

The pro-Congress reformers see ways to strengthen the committees, both in general and in relation to the executive, without impairing their autonomy. Many observers, including members of Congress, have noted the confusion and overlapping of committee jurisdictions. President Ford's 1975 energy proposals were parceled out among four House and nine Senate committees, and this dispersion of authority surely contributed to Congress' failure to formulate a comprehensive energy policy. Moreover, committee workloads are unevenly distributed; some panels have many major responsibilities while others have far less onerous burdens. A House Select Committee on Committees, recognizing these difficulties, proposed in 1974 to eliminate two committees (Post Office and Civil Service, and Internal Security) entirely and to alter significantly the jurisdictions of fourteen others [U.S.

Congress 1974]. The House rejected the plan; too many members had vested interests in the existing arrangements. Senators seem to share such sentiments, for when they created a Commision on the Operation of the Senate in 1975, they excluded the question of committee jurisdictions from its mandate. Nonetheless, clarified committee responsibility might well help Congress to capitalize on its members' energies and expertise. Realigned committees and subcommittees, especially if well staffed and supplied with information, might well prove capable of developing effective public policy.

Whether or not the system is restructured, congressional committees could benefit from improved procedures. More open, less carefully stage-managed hearings, increased opportunity for deliberation, and less constraints on the participation of rank-and-file members should permit airing of additional points of view. Improved hearings and extended consideration might produce more useful reports, which, if circulated to the full chamber well in advance of floor consideration, might help to raise the quality of debate. Such changes in committee practice, promoting wider participation and fuller discussion, could make Congress more responsive and more effective in opposing the executive.

Along with the congressional supremacists' faith in open, autonomous committees go a distrust of centralized political parties and resistance to reforms designed to achieve that end. Strengthened party caucuses or policy committees would reduce the chance for various interests, out of favor with party leaders, to be heard or to exert influence; strong parties might move too quickly, running roughshod over minorities that deserve to have a say. Accordingly, the political parties in Congress should remain loose confederations that do little more than facilitate legislative organization. The recent enlargement of the Senate Democrats' Steering Committee, which makes committee assignments, could cut in either direction: It might permit other points of view to be heard in the assignment process, or, if the new members supported the leadership—the Majority Leader chairs the Steering Committee—it might give the party additional control.[13]

The pro-Congress forces seem as satisfied with the general procedural and structural organization of the legislature as they are with autonomous committees and weak political parties. To be sure, they would prefer fuller debate in the House of Representatives and greater opportunity to propose amendments without restriction; such changes would permit a wider range of views to find expression. But they have resisted reform that might alter the fundamental character of Congress. They opposed changes in the power of the House Rules Committee and in the Senate's rule of unlimited debate that might mute minority voices or restrain minority power. The rules should, from this point of view, continue to protect decentralization of authority; current practice enhances responsiveness.

Without making fundamental changes in legislative organization or procedure, the pro-Congress reformers seek to reassert legislative prerogatives in the face of what they see as a dramatic shift toward presidential domination of the policy-making process. They have been delighted with the passage of the War Powers and Budget Reform bills and hope that such legislation does, in fact, enhance congressional participation in policy formulation.[14]

Another way the legislative supremacists would strengthen Congress is to provide the lawmakers with better staff resources and more information. Increased staffing has much to recommend it. Additional workers could generate and analyze new data; the lawmaker would get careful research support based on reliable information. Providing the minority party with its own independent staff would allow it to state its differences with the majority party more clearly and persuasively. Members of the House might be allowed to have legislative assistants comparable to those provided senators. In general, more aid might improve both the lawmakers' rationality and their ability to confront executive branch specialists.

Yet enlarged staffs, however attractive they seem in theory, may not in practice strengthen the legislature's capacity to challenge the President; indeed, some skeptics hold that more staff would create additional burdens rather than alleviate present ones. More employees might discover or create new areas for attention and, as a result, impose new demands on the already overcommitted time and energies of legislators. Too large a staff might convert a lawmaker into an office manager, to the detriment of policy-making tasks. Without proper supervision, staffers, especially investigators, might be tempted to engage in unrestrained partisanship and to neglect data gathering and idea generating.

A related set of proposals seeks to improve the quantity and the quality of information available to Congress. Insufficient and unreliable data often make it difficult for legislators to oppose bureaucratic experts; the lawmaker may feel obliged to defer to the specialists. Executive privilege—by which the President can, in the "national interest," decide to withhold information from Congress—and national defense requirements limit the data available to the legislature.[15] Interbranch competition and suspicion lead executive branch personnel to enlarge the areas in which they feel they must not release information. Moreover, the executive branch is able to put its own construction on events in a way that minimizes legislative opportunity to advance alternative proposals: Representatives of the executive branch brief the media in "off-the-record" or "not-for-attribution" sessions, releasing only that information they deem advisable to reveal, interpreting what they do make available to suit their own purposes. In addition, news, appropriately structured, can be "leaked" to the media.

Beyond these impediments to full disclosure imposed by the executive, the nature of Congress itself contributes to its information deficit. A decentralized institution, with numerous centers of autonomous power, each with lines to different information sources, leads to fragmentary, uncoordinated, or often unavailable data; data collected in one place, for one set of purposes, are simply not made accessible to other legislators in other areas with other purposes in mind. Individual lawmakers must often make decisions on complex and controversial issues with minimal information, certainly less than they would need to decide with some acceptable degree of "rationality."[16]

Two sets of proposals have emerged to remedy this grave defect in congressional deliberation and decision making. The first, and most pragmatic, seeks to remove current impediments to gaining information and to expand the presently available data sources. Congress has tried to move against the "executive privilege" doctrine; legislation has been introduced that would (1) require executive personnel to appear before legislative committees, if only to claim the privilege; (2) require a formal, written presidential statement to invoke the privilege; and (3) enforce the request for information by mandating an automatic cutoff of funds for a noncomplying agency. Such a bill would force the executive to justify withholding information from Congress.

In the meantime other steps are possible. Additional staff for research purposes—either for individual members or for committees—would help produce additional data. More funds for existing information-gathering agencies, such as the Congressional Research Service of The Library of Congress or the General Accounting Office, would enable them to investigate along more fronts and in greater depth. Learning experiences for legislators including foreign travel, on-site visits to federal installations, money to buy books and time to read, might be provided. Other proposals include extended use of outside consultants or congressionally created task forces comparable to those that the President uses, and the establishment of a "congressional institute of scholars" or some similar "university-type organization."[17]

Far more basic, and probably more promising in the long run, is a second set of proposals urging Congress to harness computerized information storage and retrieval systems. Utilization of such techniques may be necessary simply to stay abreast of the executive, notably the Defense Department, which has pioneered in using electronic equipment in policy formulation. Without adaptation in this sphere, the legislature may find its information deficit too severe ever to make up. A relatively simple and inexpensive congressional information-processing system is not out of reach [Janda 1966, 1968]. With little difficulty, all lawmakers could have on their desks a remote terminal, linked to a central computer, that they could use to call for information on topics of interest to them. This is an important point: Legislators could choose what they want to know. Their freedom to specialize, to follow their own inclinations, need not be impaired; they run little risk of being overwhelmed by information of no use to them. Their options to act consistently with political and value considerations remain open; the information system is the lawmakers' servant, not their master.

Consider how information storage and retrieval of this type could aid congressional policy making. The often arduous task of discovering the existence, content, and location of bills of interest could be vastly simplified. The computer could store a "legislative history"; at any time lawmakers could get an up-to-date status report on any measure. By working out their own position before they have to act, they reduce their dependence on word-of-mouth assurances from experts, party colleagues, or House leaders, and avoid being caught off guard. Each lawmaker would be in a far better position to interject personal views into congressional deliberations. Computerized information retrieval might also provide data on lobbyists—who they are, whom they represent, what legislation they are interested in, where to reach them, and so forth; on actions taken by the executive branch; on the results of studies undertaken by the Congressional Research Service, the General Accounting Office, or the various committee staffs; or on the contents of present law. The ready availability of information from these and other sources would enable congresspersons to make choices based on considerably more data than now enter their calculations.

In all these ways, then, Congress can be strengthened relative to the executive. Following passage of the War Powers bill, it began to reassert its control over foreign affairs. Budgetary reform, especially if linked to improved information resources, should permit the legislature to take full advantage of its power of the purse to impose its own financial priorities. In the long run, creation of new resources—expert staffs and better information—may prove more fundamental in permitting Congress to have its way, even in the face of stiff executive opposition. Increased legislative power, reflecting views that differ from those of the executive, would obviously contribute to a more responsive policy-making process.

This vision of the pro-Congress reformers, then, consists of a decentralized, responsive legislature capable of determining public policy and making its choices stick against executive opposition. As a responsive institution, a resurgent Congress could listen to a diversity of interests and blend the sentiments of numerous power holders into legislative programs that would compete on equal terms with what the executive proposes. Such competition, the interplay of roughly equal branches of government, should enhance the responsiveness of the entire policy process.

The cost of such a vision would be in the area of responsibility. The more Congress is capable of frustrating the President, the greater the possibility of deadlock. The greater the need to reach agreements through bargaining, whether within the legislature or between Congress and the executive, the less likely it is that policy will be bold or imaginative. Moreover, the greater the number of interests that any policy settlement must accommodate, the slower a decision will be in coming. Thus, a fully responsive process, open to all points of view and marked by multiple channels of communication, might produce policy of the "too little, too late" variety. It might find itself overtaken by events and outstripped by history.

AN ACCOUNTABLE CONGRESS

Regardless of whether executive or legislative supremacy seems preferable, accountability remains a desirable value, one that serves to complement either responsibility or responsiveness. As noted earlier, accountability sustains responsibility in a straightforward fashion. The electorate chooses between two political parties and in so doing gives the winner both a mandate to govern and the majority to do so. In subsequent elections the voters decide, based on their assessment of the incumbents' performance, whether to renew that mandate or to place a new party in office. Retrospective evaluation by the electorate constitutes the chief check on the administration's behavior; unless the citizenry is prepared and able to hold its rulers accountable, the power of the government would remain unlimited and unchecked.

Where responsiveness is the central concern, accountability seems both more difficult and, perhaps, less critical. A decentralized system is certainly harder for voters to fathom. When things go badly, it is difficult to know whom to blame if the fateful decisions emerge from elaborate bargaining among numerous participants at multiple stages of a complex process. The voters must pay far more attention to pin down who did what. At the same time, however, the open communications channels of a responsive Congress provide alternatives to accountability. Citizens can do more than judge ex post facto; they can, if they choose, use whatever access is available to them, as individuals or as group members, to present their views in advance. Thus, accountability, which remains desirable, is not the only mechanism of control; rather it is another way by which the electorate can seek to set national directions.

In either case, accountability provides a device by which the ruled can manage those whom they select to rule them, and steps have been proposed to remedy defects in the process (noted in Chapter 2). A first condition for accountability is that the citizens be aware of their representatives' records. Several steps seem likely to help generate more information about Congress, although not all of them are within the power of the legislature to take. For one thing, the mass media can be encouraged to provide additional congressional coverage. Admittedly, it is difficult to endow a 535-member, two-chamber institution with the aura and galmour that automatically attach to a single chief executive, but television and the press could do a better job. They could give the kind of coverage accorded to the Senate Watergate hearings and the House Judiciary Committee's impeachment hearings to other important matters, for example, the details of national health insurance or annual budget proposals. As matters now stand, only the most dramatic events receive coverage and, then, only in the most nationally oriented press, such as *The New York Times* or *The Washington Post.*

Congress cannot compel media attention, but it has, in some areas at least, made the media's task somewhat simpler by exposing more of its decision-making process to media investigations. Measures such as open hearings, recorded votes, and full disclosure of campaign financing should help the citizenry, through the media, to discover who in Congress has or has not done what with regard to public policy and, perhaps, why such actions were or were not taken.

Second, accountability requires informed, interested citizens capable of matching their own views with those of their representatives and judging them accordingly. Little direct reform is possible, but some current trends seem promising. Evidence from sample surveys shows that the better educated tend to be more aware of, concerned about, and knowledgeable about political affairs. Since educational levels are rising across the nation, more and more citizens are potentially able to exercise accountability. If these voters have the benefit of better media coverage of a less secretive Congress, they may evaluate the legislature more carefully and more knowledgeably.

Providing clear choices among candidates within single states or districts—the third prerequisite for effective accountability—is more problematic; little can be done to guarantee that voters can select from ideologically distinct nominees. Under a responsible order, this would be unnecessary. The individual candidates would be indebted to the centralized parties, and the voter would merely have to form a broad judgment as to the desirability of retaining the incumbent party. In an order emphasizing responsiveness, the parties would remain decentralized, and the availability of a politically distinct opposition candidate would depend on the uncertain operation of nominating politics in a given constituency.

Accountability, in short, will not be improved easily. However much the observers may wish for more media attention to Congress or for more citizen concern with the legislature and the issues it confronts, there is not much the reformer can do. About all that is possible, and Congress has moved in this direction, is to make sure that those who wish to inform themselves are not thwarted by unnecessary secrecy in the legislative branch. Greater numbers of interested citizens attuned to a more visible Congress give rise to the hope for more accountability.

SUMMARY

Because recent reform efforts have been inconsistent—stressing change to foster responsibility, responsiveness, and accountability—reformers continue to project a future featuring one or another "pure" or abstract vision of Congress. Two constrasting and somewhat incompatible, perspectives characterize these visions. Those who put a high premium on prompt, efficient solutions to policy problems seek to move toward a more centralized legislature. They are prepared to sacrifice openness and multiple channels of communication—that is, responsiveness—in favor of effective resolution of policy issues—that is, responsibility. They propose numerous reforms, outlined above, to this end, and they are prepared to rely on citizen-enforced accountability to keep the powerful executive in check. On the other side are those, equally committed to reform, who place the ultimate value on a free, open deliberative process. As the price for responsiveness they are prepared to endure a decentralized scheme of things, seemingly irresponsible, that reaches decisions slowly and only after considerable negotiation and compromise. They, too, propose a variety of reforms, also outlined above. Although they do not oppose it, they rely less on accountability after the fact than on the ability of individual citizens or organized groups to present their views prior to policy formulation. There is, of course, no way to choose between these alternative visions of Congress' future on definitive or empirical grounds; the choice ultimately must rest on normative grounds, on the relative weight any observer assigns to the competing values of responsibility and responsiveness.

Notes

1. Indeed, there has been an upsurge of interest in congressional reform. For fuller treatments and discussions of reform issues see Bolling 1965; Clark 1965; Davidson et al. 1966; U.S. Congress 1973; and Ornstein 1974, 1975b.

2. The discussion of reformist perspectives must, of necessity, be oversimplified. The effort here is to identify major points of view, but it must be recognized that there are multiple variations on each theme that cannot be clearly differentiated here because of space limitations.

3. For arguments supporting a "strong" or dominant presidency, see Dahl 1950, Lippmann 1954, and Rossiter 1960. On the responsible party idea, see Burns 1949 and 1963; American Political Science Association 1950; and Broder 1972. On the latter notion, see also Kirkpatrick 1971, and Pomper 1971.

4. In fact, Butler [1955] and McKenzie [1964] suggest that British parties scarcely resemble the image held by the responsible party school.

5. For instance, new rules might eliminate or curtail (1) the "morning hour," when Senators make short speeches and handle miscellaneous chores not immediately related to lawmaking; (2) the practice of insisting that the *Journal* be read in full; and (3) the dilatory use of repeated quorum calls.

6. Filibusters can begin at numerous points: on the motion to take up (begin consideration of) a bill, on amendments, on passage, and on acceptance of conference report. Reformers have proposed making the motion to take up a bill nondebatable, thus removing one opportunity to talk a bill to death.

7. The Voting Rights Act of 1970 is typical of the successful operation of this strategy. Congress appended a provision granting 18-year-olds the right to vote, despite President Nixon's announced view that such a change required a constitutional amendment. The President signed the measure reluctantly and sought an early court test of the constitutionality of changing the voting age by statute. Also, as noted above, the legal end to American military involvement in Southeast Asia came about, in 1973, as a result of a partially successful application of the strategy.

8. Of course, this system requires that the electorate have command of the political issues, and there is some doubt that, as presently constituted, it is capable of this. We will return to the problem below.

9. Diffusion of authority is highly compatible with the legislator's career aspirations. In a stable institution like Congress, many lawmakers covet long-term service; they seek reelection regularly. Thus, structural and procedural changes that serve to open avenues to power, even over small segments of legislative business, allow legislators to make a mark and to find a niche early in their congressional service.

10. There was a fear that, through reapportionment, conservative rural area would lose representation to the liberal cities. This fear seems largely to have been misplaced. Now that the dust of the *Baker v. Carr* and *Wesberry v. Sanders* decisions has settled, it appears that the dozen or so seats in the House of Representatives that rural areas lost wound up controlled by suburban conservatives rather than by the urban liberals. The impact of court-enforced reapportionment has been minimal to date. Should the courts proceed to encourage or demand creation of districts to assure

minorities—blacks in central cities, for instance—
representation in Congress, the fears of the pro-
Congress forces might be realized. It is highly unlikely
that the present "Nixon-Burger" Supreme Court will
move in this direction.

11. In the 94th Congress, when seniority ceased to be
binding, there was no centralization. The Democratic
leaders—Speaker Carl Albert (Okla.) and Majority
Leader Thomas P. O'Neill (Mass.)—recommended the
senior member of each committee be given the chair.
The Steering and Policy Committee recommended
ousting two senior chairmen—Wright Patman and
Wayne Hays. The caucus restored Hays but deprived
H. R. Poage and F. Edward Hébert, as well as Patman,
of their chairs. This process can scarcely be described
as centralized.

12. The prospect of domination of the committee assignment process by party leadership might be more real if
the same party controlled the White House and Congress; under such circumstances the leaders might be
tempted to place presidential loyalists in important
assignments. Leaders capable of controlling committee action by manipulating panel membership would,
of course, tend to centralize power in the House.

13. In 1973 the newly enlarged Steering Committee did
manipulate the membership of the Finance Committee, adding liberals in what appeared to be an effort to
weaken the position of the committee's chairman,
Russell Long (La.). Two years later, the Steering
Committee placed two more liberals on Finance, three
on Armed Services, and, in a head-to-head confronta-
tion, James Abourezk (S.D.), rather than conservative
James B. Allen (Ala.), on the Judiciary Committee.

These incidents suggest that the Steering Committee may support the party leaders.

14. The new budget procedures may not necessarily offer a gain in responsiveness. On one hand, the reforms may enable the congressional point of view to prevail against the President's in the allocation of financial resources; legislative decisions, as responsive choices, may well reflect sentiments other than the executive's. On the other hand, the reformed budgetary process seems likely to cut into the power of the congressional committees. The panels will remain open and responsive since they will continue to authorize funds through a negotiation process, but they will be seriously constrained by overall spending ceilings. That is, they will have to bargain about a limited sum and will not be able to accommodate multiple interests simply by increasing the total funds allocated. The most responsive sort of bill, the "something-for-everything" logrolling type, will be severely restricted. So the new system may strengthen Congress as a whole in its struggle with the executive and may make the ultimate outcomes more responsive to congressional preferences, but at the same time it may lead to internal centralization with the Budget Committees exercising authority formerly held by the committees and subcommittees.

15. In *U.S. v. Nixon* (1974) the Supreme Court required the defendant to turn over to the Special Prosecutor some tapes that Nixon asserted were protected by executive privilege. Often overlooked in that decision, however, is the seeming defense of the executive privilege principle. While not applicable in instances involving possible criminal misconduct, executive privilege, the Court seemed to say, did have many

useful purposes. The implication was that the principle might well be properly applied in other more ordinary circumstances.

16. For a cogent discussion of Congress' information problems and some proposed remedies, see Saloma 1969.

17. On some of these notions, see Dechert 1966 and Robinson 1966. In 1975, a private organization, with the support of several members of Congress, undertook to set up an institute of scholars to do research for the legislature.

5.

Toward Majoritarian Democracy in Congress

THESE ALTERNATIVE VISIONS ARE, IN A SENSE, illusory. The proposals they describe are intended to move Congress toward greater responsibility or toward increased responsiveness, but they do not represent fullblown, widely shared visions of a better political order. Rather, they denote tendencies—toward a more powerful executive or a revived legislature—that seem most likely to improve the political system. Within these broad visions, there remains considerable controversy about the wisdom and desirability of specific reforms. Those who advocate a stronger President or a strengthened Congress often do not agree on the precise steps that will achieve their goal. It is unlikely that widespread agreement on any package of fundamental reforms will develop in such an atmosphere. Change is more likely to come, as it has in the past: incrementally in response to specific crises or particular problems.

It is in this spirit that the concluding section of this book advances a vision of a congressional future called "majoritarian democracy." This proposal takes off from the 1971–1975 reforms, utilizing the best of them to obtain a useful mix of responsibility and responsiveness and a balance between the twin needs for deliberation and decisiveness. This modest proposal may satisfy no one; it may picture a policy-making process too slow to be responsible, too centralized to be responsive. Yet it seems clear that no fully responsible and responsive political order is possible. While both values have their assets, they are sufficiently exclusive that a gain in one is likely to bring about a loss in the other. The intention in this proposal is to maximize both values.

Such a mixed pattern seems desirable because neither the executive-supremacy nor the legislative-supremacy position is tenable. The advocacy of executive force apparently grew out of a misplaced, perhaps naive faith in the inherent goodness of the President. In the 1950s it may well have been reasonable to assume, given the political forces then operative, that only the chief executive would pursue policies of internationalism in foreign affairs and liberalism on the domestic scene. But events of the past decade have tarnished the vision of executive nobility. Presidential domination of the nation's Vietnam policy and the Watergate era's revelations about Richard Nixon's behavior (the latter ironically demonstrating the thirst for power of a chief executive publicly committed to reducing the size and scope of federal government authority and activity) make clear the extent to which presidential power has grown. Not many liberals would approve executive supremacy used for such ends; it appears equally doubtful that conservatives would be eager to see such strength in the hands of a liberal in the White House. Thus, no matter whose political ox is gored, there seems good reason to avoid an undue concentration of authority in the executive's hands.[1]

Yet the congressional-supremacy arguments are no more promising or appealing. Neither a highly centralized Congress, independent of the President and capable of responsible action, nor a largely fragmented institution, totally responsive, presents a pleasing vision. The former possibility is both unrealistic (there are simply too many subjects to be handled with dispatch) and undesirable (the same arguments that apply to a powerful presidency militate against a concentration of authority in the legislature). Discontinuing federal programs to permit easier congressional dominance of those that remain seems impractical. There are too many programs, each with its own clientele, to permit easy termination; in addition, it is by no means certain that state and local governments could handle these burdens should they be devolved from the federal level. The second formulation, the open institution with minorities protected at every stage of the decision-making process, recalls the sort of paralysis, the *immobilisme*, that crippled and eventually brought down the French Fourth Republic. In short, there is little reason to expect beneficial results from converting Congress to either an exclusively responsible or an exclusively responsive institution.

The answer, quite clearly, is some combination of features that maximizes both responsibility and responsiveness. The proposal that follows is one vision of such a combination. It would wed an open, responsive, deliberative stage of legislative policy making to a more decisive, responsible decision-making phase. The former is democratic: It seeks to open avenues of participation for all, inside and outside Congress. The latter is majoritarian: It endeavors to permit majorities, given sufficient time to form, to prevail at the point of decision.

It should be made clear that what follows is in no way intended to minimize the importance of popular accountability. Accountability is highly desirable, and the steps, noted above, to make it more effective should be pursued. That is, the media should be encouraged to cover Congress fully and at length, and the legislature should follow up on the recent changes that, in general, minimize congressional secrecy.[2] There is not much that can be done to promote clear electoral choices. Given the rejection of some form of centralization of the national party under executive domination, there is little likelihood that the fragmented electoral races, with each contest virtually distinct from every other contest, can or will be altered. About all that can be done is to press candidates to present their views with some specificity, enabling the watchful, issue-oriented citizen to vote intelligently. To the extent that Congress operates more openly and the public is more attentive to the legislature, accountability is enhanced, the linkage between rulers and ruled is tightened, and the prospect for popular control of government is improved.

RESPONSIVENESS IN THE DELIBERATIVE STAGE

In the early stages of lawmaking, when the policy process should be most responsive, citizens should have ample opportunity to present their views. They should be able to suggest to Congress what they would like to see done. (Later, accountability operates and they can render, in the polling booth, a verdict about what was done.[3]) To foster responsiveness in Congress, the pro-legislative reforms are intended to democratize Congress: to get responsive individuals into the legislature and to let them speak there for the widest diversity of interests.

In electoral terms, this means continuation of present electoral arrangements. Current apportionment, reflecting population equality, is satisfactory; so is "localism," with its constituency-based, individualized campaigns. On the other hand, campaign reforms that favor incumbents are undesirable. Incumbents have vast campaign advantages—observers estimate that their congressional perquisites are worth $480,000 a year—and need little additional help. It is possible, though it is too early to be sure, that the 1974 Campaign Finance Act seriously handicaps challengers, even though the Supreme Court struck down its spending limitations. The bill's strict contribution limits may prevent challengers from raising sufficient funds to mount effective campaigns against entrenched incumbents. In any case, the electoral process should operate to allow as wide a latitude as possible for candidates who speak for local interests and voice diverging concerns.

Inside Congress, majoritarian democracy calls for a moderately paced deliberative stage that promotes the expression of multiple points of view. At the committee level, members should be assigned to the panels that will enable them to serve their constituencies best. The changes in Senate and House committee assignment procedures and the limitations on filling subcommittee chairs should serve to diffuse power, giving junior legislators greater opportunities to achieve positions of some significance. More important, perhaps, and at variance with more commonly proposed reforms, committee responsiveness could be extended by ensuring, as the 1970 Reorganization Act intended, that panel majorities could firmly control the conduct of committee business. Under such conditions, there would be less concern about the mode of selecting chairpersons; it is not seniority that has been at the root of most complaints, but rather the fact that the system automatically elevates the most senior majority member to a very *powerful* position. If the committee leader were more equal in power to the other members of the committee, the real virtue of seniority—the automatic, noncompetitive character of the choice of chairman—might be preserved.

Such democratically governed legislative committees could consider the available options to each bill more fully if information and research resources were enlarged. Extra staff, but not so many that the congressperson becomes an office manager rather than a policy maker, seems likely to help; enlarged minority staff would certainly aid in airing additional points of view. So, too, would the creation and use of a computerized information retrieval system; legislators would be able to generate and sustain their own policy proposals to a far greater extent than is now possible. Finally, responsiveness would be served more if committees with clear jurisdictions conducted open hearings—scheduled well in advance, with ample notice given to potential witnesses, and importantly, with the less well-organized interests invited, encouraged, and perhaps even subsidized to appear.

In short, majoritarian democracy envisions the continuation of a fragmented congressional decision process, featuring independent, specialized committees as the basis of the division of labor. The reforms suggested above are designed to make sure that the widest possible range of opinion finds its way into legislative deliberations. Norms acknowledging specialization of, and reciprocity among, committees will continue to be observed. Political parties will, likewise, continue for the most part as nonideological facilitators of election and legislative organization. Under such conditions, legislative committees composed of expert and well-informed lawmakers, adequately staffed and open to the views of all interested parties, should generate responsive policy.

RESPONSIBILITY: FACILITATING POLICY MAKING

However responsive the process by which legislation is formulated, such legislation must have a chance not only to pass Congress but also to survive executive branch opposition. Otherwise, of course, the legislative process is an exercise in futility. Unless the national legislature can act, and act in ways that do resolve problems, it is not likely ever to serve as an effective counterweight to executive authority. Action on two fronts is desirable to this end: internal change to permit majorities to act and statutory restraints on presidential power.

On the first front, changes should permit what the responsive deliberative phase has produced to be voted up or down with a minimum of delay. This requires removal of several procedural devices that serve to protect minorities and that slow down or block congressional action. The main focus here is on changing the rules to facilitate majoritarian action. In the House of Representatives several reforms would help guarantee prompter dispatch of committee recommendations. Extended panel consideration of proposals, often intended to bury the legislation permanently, could be prevented by a more usable discharge rule. After allowing sufficient time for full study and deliberation, say 90 or 120 days, a discharge petition bearing 150 signatures would enable bills to move to the floor for a vote.[4]

A similar change in the Rules Committee would be in order. Most observers recognize the need for a "traffic cop" to regulate the flow of floor business, but trouble develops when the Rules panel uses its power to block bills that the standing committees wish to send to the floor. As a remedy, permanent adoption of the 21-Day Rule, which has twice been enacted temporarily, would guarantee the full chamber a chance to pass on reported legislation; Rules could only interpose a three-week delay in getting the bill to the floor. Such a move would obviate the need to rely on the party leaders to move legislation. Other minor changes aimed at eliminating the use of delaying tactics— excessive quorum calls, reading the *Journal* in full, and so on—would make marginal improvements in the House's ability, already far superior to that of the Senate, to deal decisively with pending bills.

As noted, the major target for reform in the upper chamber has been the filibuster. The new cloture rule, especially if coupled with changes eliminating the "morning hour," making debate germane and focused, and limiting the opportunity for filibusters, should move floor proceedings more quickly toward a decision point. These Senate changes, like those proposed for the House, would increase the likelihood that determined majorities could carry the day on behalf of the bills they favored.[5]

These bills would, of course, have to survive competition with the President, who could still veto measures and prevail unless Congress could muster a two-thirds majority in each house to override the veto. Still, some reforms, recently enacted, should enhance the competitive position of the legislature; of these, budgetary reform is the most important. The imposition by Congress of a spending ceiling in line with anticipated revenue, and allocation of that overall sum to various budgetary categories—all prepared with the help of substantially improved staff and information resources—should make legislative budget choices serious competitors to those that the executive makes. Moreover, the anti-impoundment features of the bill, requiring the executive to release funds unless the legislature agrees to his action, should ensure that congressional fiscal priorities will prevail more often.

Legislation defining and regularizing the claim of executive privilege and requiring agencies to divulge information would reduce the information deficiency under which Congress operates. The recently enacted war powers legislation, delimiting the President's authority to commit military forces in "undeclared wars" or "police actions" without legislative approval, should restore some congressional voice in the determination of foreign policy. All these laws could help to redress the executive-legislative imbalance of power in the favor of Congress; all could contribute to a policy process in which both branches were forces to reckon with.

NEEDED: A NEW CONGRESSIONAL IMAGE

Statutory and structural changes, however much they would strengthen Congress against the President, are not adequate alone to bring about an effective majoritarian democratic institution. More subtle change, more difficult to achieve; is required: Congress must enhance its reputation as a body committed to placing national above local interests, an institution whose integrity is beyond question and which can rise above "politics as usual" to make contributions to the national welfare equal, if not superior, to those of the executive. Congress suffers in this regard, for it tends to be assessed more as an appendage to than as a rival of the President. When the public holds the chief executive in high esteem, it usually values the legislature as well; when the President's prestige falls, so does that of Congress [Davidson et al. 1966].

Competing for public respect with the unitary executive is not easy for the plural legislature. Yet some of the reforms outlined above may help enhance Congress' reputation. More media attention, less internal secrecy, and more forceful imposition of congressional views in policy making may help citizens to realize that the legislature *is* an important feature of the political landscape. A major cause of public skepticism is a sense that lawmakers are not entirely ethical. Doubts about the detachment of legislators have led to proposals to ensure that they are as free as possible from conflicts of interest and that their actions are intended to advance the public good, not their own financial positions. To the extent that doubts about freedom from self-serving behavior exist the reputation of Congress and popular support for its views will be eroded.

The increasing number of cases of legislators engaging in illegal or unethical actions in the past decade has heightened the concern over ethics. But the pressures of legislative life contribute to a situation in which ethics are constantly at issue. On one hand, public expectations are high; the citizens seem to believe that their elected representatives must be beyond reproach. On the other hand, to put it bluntly, legislators need money. They must engage in virtually continuous campaigning, which is costly. Some maintain residences both in their constituency and in Washington. Some are caught up in the demanding social life of the capital, with its expensive entertaining. In addition, the nature of the lawmaking task creates difficulties. The notion that Congress should be responsive and stay in touch with the populace requires that lawmakers listen to the requests and petitions of many groups and organizations. It is not surprising that those with policy concerns seek to exploit their access to lawmakers to further their own goals; in so doing they may sometimes offer inducements that fall between outright corruption—graft and bribery—and a legitimate campaign contribution.

In recent years there have been criminal indictments against several legislators for illegal acts committed during their terms in office. Ex-Senator Daniel Brewster (D., Md.), former House members Thomas Johnson (D., Md.), John Dowdy (D., Tex.), and J. Irwin Whalley (R., Pa.), and Representative Bertram Podell (D., N.Y.) have been indicted for or convicted of corrupt practices. The Senate censured Thomas Dodd (D., Conn.) for misuse of campaign funds in 1967. The House excluded Adam Clayton Powell (D., N.Y.) following a series of legal problems, including Powell's refusal to pay a libel judgment against him. In 1973 Representative William O. Mills (R., Md.) committed suicide after the publication of reports that he had received an illegal $25,000 cash contribution to his campaign; and in 1975 George V. Hansen (R., Ind.) pleaded guilty to, and Andrew J. Hinshaw (R., Cal.) was convicted of, campaign finance law violations.

Far more pervasive, however, than these dramatic events are conflict of interest situations in which lawmakers render judgments on matters in which they have a personal stake. How is the public to regard Congress when Representative Robert T. Watkins (R., Pa.), with a personal interest in the trucking business, sits on the House Commerce Committee, which has jurisdiction over the laws and the agency (the Interstate Commerce Commission) that regulate truckers? What should the popular evaluation be of Senator George Murphy (R., Calif.) when he receives a $20,000 annual retainer, a travel credit card, and half the rent on his apartment from a major corporation as compensation for "public relations" work?[6]

Such questions, asked more frequently of late, have encouraged Congress to raise its own standards of conduct. Each chamber now has a Select Committee on Standards and Conduct charged with policing the ethics of its members. According to critics, however, neither has accomplished much; both incentive and enforcement powers have been lacking. There are also a set of conflict-of-interest statutes, last revised in 1962, that outlaw bribery and corruption; proscribe compensation for appearances by legislators before federal agencies; ban direct contact between federal agencies and legislators who, as lawyers, are representing clients; and prohibit receipt of salary from an outside source as direct compensation for services rendered. Finally, there is also on the books a set of financial disclosure requirements intended to reveal the lawmakers' major sources of outside income and, thus, to expose areas of potential conflict of interest. There are limits to the operation of these statutes,[7] but they do enable the interested citizen to discover some of the possible conflicts of interest under which national lawmakers work.

To be held in high regard, especially in the more cynical post-Watergate era, Congress should be, in Dwight Eisenhower's pithy phrase, "cleaner than a hound's tooth," and critics feel that some scouring is required on the ethical front. They are unwilling to accept the present internal arrangements, especially the weak, mostly unenforceable code of ethics, or to rely exclusively on the electorate to control wrong-doing and punish transgressors.[8] The new campaign finance law, an outgrowth of Watergate, may prove helpful; it will limit the sum any individual can contribute and require full reporting and disclosure of who gives what to whom. Other proposals include a more strongly worded, more thoroughly implemented code of ethics; an expanded set of conflict of interest statutes with broad self-denying ordinances[9]; and an extension of the prohibition on receiving outside compensation to cover not only direct payment for representing an outside interest in any proceeding, including lawmaking, before the government, but also indirect payment in the form of bonuses, stock options, and the like.

There have been numerous calls for disclosure laws under which every lawmaker would make annual public reports of outside income. Senator Clifford Case (R., N.J.) *he was defeated* has for a number of years pushed to require each member of Congress to reveal the donors of all gifts, including campaign contributions; to report all income from outside sources; to issue an assets-and-liabilities statement; and to record all sales and purchases of stocks, bonds, and real estate. The argument for disclosure rests on the extraordinary difficulty in establishing when genuine conflict of interest exists. It is certainly possible for legislators to share viewpoints with their constituents, or some segment of them, and to act on behalf of those interests without engaging in improper conduct. The line between public and private interest, in other words, is not easy to draw precisely, and disclosure laws would have the virtue of revealing what financial stakes members have in issues they must decide.

In short, if Congress is to compete on equal terms with the executive, and to make its policy determinations prevail, it must have the support of the public; it must be recognized as a non–self-serving body whose priorities are not suspect. To this end, codes of conduct, conflict of interest statutes, and disclosure laws should help convince the citizenry that the legislature has nothing to hide and thereby raise the popular esteem so necessary for a strong national legislature.

At last, and perhaps most important, requisite for a Congress capable of independent policy making is the will and determination to assert its preferences. Critics often charge, and with some justice, that many lawmakers are unwilling to run the risks of serious commitment to policy making. They prefer, so the argument runs, to concern themselves with local interests and let the President set the legislative workload. Congress has often been less than a forceful proponent for its own legislative initiatives. The Democratic majority in the 94th Congress seemed prepared to take on a politically weakened executive, but the exercise of congressional will, if it is to mean anything, must become common practice in more normal political circumstances as well. Until recently at least, Congress tolerated a set of internal norms, customs, and folkways that placed minority power and inaction, through reciprocity and courtesy, above majority rule and decisiveness. Congress has put itself in a position of self-protection, where it can take credit for what goes right and avoid the blame for unsuccessful policy formulation. If Congress is to move toward more effective policy making, it must overcome the tendency to avoid risk and to defer to the executive or other experts rather than to stand and fight for its own preferences.

What is required is a Congress co-equal, in more than just a theoretical sense, with the President, a legislature willing to assert its views and to accept the consequences when its actions prove unsuccessful. This necessitates a shift in the psychological outlook of many legislators. They must be prepared to adopt publicly a national posture on issues even when local considerations might suggest some other course of action. They must eschew a legislative culture that puts a premium on "something for everyone" and seeks this goal through reciprocity and "logrolling"[10]; rather they must be prepared to say "no" to a colleague and, more difficult, to hear "no" said to them. Members of Congress must be willing to match their best efforts against the ideas of the executive and to stand or fall on the quality of those efforts. This requires risk taking and political courage. Such a show of determination will not come easily, and there will unquestionably be electoral casualties along the way. Yet only if such an exercise of will is made can Congress hope to achieve parity with a powerful executive.

SUMMARY

Majoritarian democracy envisions an operative system of checks and balances. More precisely, it projects a system of separate institutions, legislative and executive, sharing overlapping powers. The view assumes that the older, now seemingly naive, faith in the beneficence of the President is untenable, and that some executive-legislative partnership in policy making is desirable. Such cooperative arrangements, from the legislative point of view at least, include three major components:

1. *A responsive deliberative phase of policy making.* Policy formulation would reflect a democratic, participatory process. A strengthened legislature, with better staff and information resources and open to all interested points of view, would sift proposals and come up with legislation designed to serve the nation's needs. There would, of course, be costs involved. Such a careful, reflective, and open deliberative stage would take time and would create intervals during which problems might intensify or opportunities for solutions might be lost. Yet such a price must be paid if our politics are to be responsive, if solutions are to reflect citizen wants, needs, and desires. Moreover, the costs can be minimized if the deliberative stage is not allowed to drag on beyond all reasonable necessity.

2. *A responsible decision-making phase of policy making.* The deliberative stage would give way to a decisive, action phase of decision making. After some proper interval, committed legislators should have produced some legislation for consideration by the full chamber. At this time, Congress should be organized, in a majoritarian fashion, to make decisions. Easier discharge of bills from committee; simpler access to the floor, especially through limitations placed on the House Rules Committee; more germane debate, especially in the Senate; elimination of delaying tactics, most particularly the filibuster in the upper chamber—all these should permit simple majorities to act. After due deliberation and careful formulation, bills should be judged on the merits and voted up or down without delay.

There are costs here, too. To move legislation ahead, with dispatch if possible, means foreclosing opportunities to defeat by indirection. Minorities can and should have a full say during the deliberative stage, but at the point of action they must be restrained; they must not be permitted to make policy by blocking decision making. At this stage, the need to act, to be responsible, must override the need to represent, to be responsive. Congress must first listen, and listen carefully; then it must act, and do so decisively.

3. *A strengthened Congress relative to the executive.* Congressional policy making, reflecting a satisfactory mix of responsiveness and responsibility, must produce decisions that have a reasonable chance of prevailing against presidential power. The present proposal envisages a combination of increased statutory authority, a revived congressional reputation that is rooted in greater openness and a clearly visible increase in ethical standards, and an enlarged reservoir of determination to make legislative priorities competitive.

Continued reform in these directions would go far
ward demonstrating such a determination on the pa
Congress. Throughout the entire process, the pu
more aware of and better informed about the le
ture, would be preparing to render judgment an
Congress accountable at the ensuing election.

Even though these proposals can be adopte
mentally and without major constitutional alteration, the
prospects for reform are uncertain. The executive will,
needless to say, resist such changes; some in the legislature may be reluctant to yield powers they presently possess. Vietnam and Watergate have perhaps provided the
necessary impetus for change: They have revealed how
strong the President has become, especially in relation to
Congress, and have given Congress the opportunity to
move against a relatively weak executive. Majoritarian
democracy presents a vision of Congress and a
President—each with its own constituency and independent power base—working together to make responsible
and responsive public policy, subject to popular accountability. If this picture is attractive, then Congress must
continue to build on the 1971–1975 reforms. The reinvig-
oration of the legislature depends on such action.

Notes

1. As a practical matter, the kinds of changes necessary to implement a presidential supremacy arrangement, especially with responsible parties, would require amending the Constitution and making numerous statutory revisions. Congress can hardly be expected to enact the dissolution of its own claims to policy-making influence.

2. Admittedly, not all legislative activity can or should go on in public. "Open covenants, openly arrived at" is no more valid in Congress than in diplomacy. Topics like national security demand secrecy, and compromise settlements may well be more easily worked out in private. What is important is that the public be in a position to find out what has been done and who supported these actions.

3. Voting simultaneously fosters accountability and responsiveness. As a retrospective judgment, it holds incumbents to account for their past performance. Looking ahead, it offers suggestions about what should be done in the future; at least it does so if policy sentiments shape voters' choices. In this section, the act of voting is treated as a means of transmitting views on political issues.

4. One of the chief reasons for the relative infrequency with which discharge petitions (requiring 218 signatures, a majority of the full House) are used is the reluctance of rank-and-file members to risk the wrath of powerful committee leaders by signing the petitions. Easier discharge requirements coupled with a relaxation of the chairperson's control over a committee should increase the prospect of getting legislation to the floor.

5. These majorities would be similar to those found at present—shifting from issue to issue and created as a result of a negotiating process.

6. For numerous other examples and a discussion of conflict of interest in the contemporary Congress, see Sherrill 1970.

7. Members of the House publicly reveal the businesses from which they receive income in excess of $1000 annually or in which their holdings are valued at $5000 or more, *if* the source of income was engaged in "substantial" business with the federal government or was under federal regulation; they also report their connections with organizations from which they receive an income of $1000 or more. The public disclosures of senators are limited to lecture fees and honoraria; all fees are to be reported. Legislators also file additional data, but these remain sealed and are opened only under extraordinary circumstances.

8. The voters do seem to respond to charges of unethical conduct on occasion. In 1966, charges that Senator A. Willis Robertson (D., Va.), Chairman of the Senate Banking and Currency Committee, was too close to banking interests may have contributed to his defeat. Robertson sponsored legislation to provide an exemption from the antitrust laws for two banks that desired to merge; the bank responded by sending out letters urging stockholders to give their "thanks" to Robertson, presumably in the form of campaign contributions. Two years later, Senator Edward Long (D., Mo.), was retired from office following *Life* magazine's report that he had received substantial sums from the Teamsters Union for "referral fees."

9. For instance, the New York City Bar Association [1970] has proposed to prohibit, effective six years after election, the practice of law by sitting legislators and to bar members' law firms from representing clients that the members cannot serve. Other reformers seek a post-employment ban, like that imposed on former executive employees, on ex-legislators' dealings with the federal government. For a summary of many of these issues of ethics, see Getz 1966.

10. Mayhew [1966] suggests the Democrats in the House of Representatives derive considerable party cohesion from reciprocity. Each faction of the party seems ideologically flexible and quite prepared to provide support for colleagues on matters of concern to them in return for backing on items of importance to itself. Such a habit (not found among House Republicans) would be difficult to break.

Bibliography

American Political Science Association, Committee on Political Parties, *Toward a More Responsible Two-Party System*. Rinehart, 1950.

Raymond A. Bauer, Ithiel de Sola Pool, and Lewis A. Dexter, *American Business and Public Policy*, 2nd ed. Aldine-Atherton, 1972.

Richard Bolling, *House Out of Order*. Dutton, 1965.

Richard W. Boyd, "Popular Control of Public Policy: A Normal Vote Analysis of the 1968 Election." *American Political Science Review*, 1972, 66:429–449.

David S. Broder, *The Party's Over: The Failure of Politics in America*. Harper & Row, 1972.

James Burnham, *Congress and the American Tradition*. Regnery, 1959.

James M. Burns, *Congress on Trial*. Harper, 1949.

James M. Burns, *The Deadlock of Democracy*. Prentice-Hall, 1963.

David Butler, "American Myths About British Political Parties." *Virginia Quarterly Review*, 1955, 31:45–56.

Angus Campbell, Philip E. Converse, Warren E. Miller, and Donald E. Stokes, *The American Voter*. Wiley, 1960.

Angus Campbell, Philip E. Converse, Warren E. Miller, and Donald E. Stokes, *Elections and the Political Order*. Wiley, 1966.

Joseph S. Clark, ed., *Congressional Reform: Problems and Prospects*. Crowell, 1965.

Congressional Quarterly Weekly Report, March 4, 1972; April 28, 1973; October 12, 1974; June 28, 1975; January 10, 1976; and February 7, 1976.

Robert A. Dahl, *Congress and Foreign Policy*. Harcourt, Brace & World, 1950.

Roger H. Davidson, David M. Kovenock, and Michael K. O'Leary, *Congress in Crisis: Politics and Congressional Reform*. Wadsworth, 1966.

Raymond H. Dawson, "Congressional Innovation and Intervention in Defense Policy: Legislative Authorization of Weapons Systems." *American Political Science Review*, 1962, 56:42–57.

Charles R. Dechert, "Availability of Information for Congressional Operations." In Alfred de Grazia, ed., *Congress: The First Branch of Government*. American Enterprise Institute, 1966.

Alfred de Grazia, *Republic in Crisis: Congress against the Executive Force*. Federal Legal Publications, 1965.

Lewis A. Dexter, "Congressmen and the Making of Military Policy." In Robert L. Peabody and Nelson W. Polsby, eds., *New Perspectives on the House of Representatives*. Rand McNally, 1963.

Lewis A. Dexter, *How Organizations Are Represented in Washington*. Bobbs-Merrill, 1969.

Jeff Fishel, *Party and Opposition*. McKay, 1973.

Lewis A. Froman, Jr., *The Congressional Process: Strategies, Rules and Procedures*. Little, Brown, 1967.

Lewis A. Froman, Jr. and Randall B. Ripley, "Conditions for Party Leadership: The Case of the House Democrats." *American Political Science Review*, 1965, 59:52–63.

Robert S. Getz, *Congressional Ethics*. Van Nostrand, 1966.

Marjorie Randon Hershey, *The Making of Campaign Strategy*. Lexington, 1974.

Abraham Holtzman, *Legislative Liaison: Executive Leadership in Congress.* Rand McNally, 1970.

Samuel P. Huntington, "Congressional Responses to the Twentieth Century." In David B. Truman, ed., *The Congress and America's Future*, 2nd ed. Prentice-Hall, 1973.

Kenneth Janda, "Information Systems for Congress." In Alfred de Grazia, ed., *Congress: The First Branch of Government*, American Enterprise Institute, 1966.

Kenneth Janda, *Information Retrieval: Applications in Political Science.* Bobbs-Merrill, 1968.

Malcolm E. Jewell and Samuel C. Patterson, *The Legislative Process in the United States*, 2nd ed. Random House, 1973.

Charles O. Jones, "Inter-party Competition for Congressional Seats." *Western Political Quarterly*, 1964, 17:461–476.

William J. Keefe and Morris S. Ogul, *The American Legislative Process*, 3rd ed. Prentice-Hall, 1973.

John W. Kingdon, *Candidates for Office.* Random House, 1968.

Evron M. Kirkpatrick, "Toward a More Responsible Two-Party System: Political Science, Policy Science or Pseudo-Science?" *American Political Science Review*, 1971, 65:965–990.

David A. Leuthold, *Electioneering in a Democracy: Campaigns for Congress.* Wiley, 1968.

Walter Lippmann, *The Public Philosophy.* Little, Brown, 1954.

David R. Mayhew, *Party Loyalty Among Congressmen: The Difference Between Democrats and Republicans.* Harvard University Press, 1966.

David R. Mayhew, Congress: The Electoral Connection. Yale University Press, 1974.

Robert T. McKenzie, British Political Parties. Praeger, 1964.

Lester W. Milbrath, The Washington Lobbyists. Rand McNally, 1963.

Richard E. Neustadt, Presidential Power. Wiley, 1960.

New York City Bar Association, Report of the Special Committee on Congressional Ethics, Congress and the Public Trust. Atheneum, 1970.

Norman J. Ornstein, ed., "Changing Congress: The Committee System." The Annals of the American Academy of Political and Social Science, 1974, 411: entire issue.

Norman J. Ornstein, "Causes and Consequences of Congressional Change: Subcommittee Reforms in the House of Representatives, 1970–73." In Norman J. Ornstein, ed., Congress in Change: Evolution and Reform. Praeger, 1975a.

Norman J. Ornstein, ed., Congress in Change: Evolution and Reform. Praeger, 1975b.

Norman J. Ornstein and David W. Rohde, "The Strategy of Reform: Recorded Teller Voting in the House of Representatives." Paper presented at the 1974 Annual Meeting of the Midwest Political Science Association.

Nelson W. Polsby, "The Institutionalization of the House of Representatives." American Political Science Review, 1968, 62:144–168.

Gerald M. Pomper, "Toward a More Responsible Two-Party System? What, Again?" Journal of Politics, 1971, 33:916–940.

Gerald M. Pomper, "From Confusion to Clarity: Issues and American Voters, 1956–1968." *American Political Science Review*, 1972, 66:415–428.

David RePass, "Issue Salience and Party Choice." *American Political Science Review*, 1971, 65:389–400.

Leroy N. Rieselbach, *Congressional Politics*. McGraw-Hill, 1973.

James A. Robinson, "Decision-Making in Congress." In Alfred de Grazia, ed., *Congress: The First Branch of Government*. American Enterprise Institute, 1966.

Clinton Rossiter, *The American Presidency*, rev. ed. Harcourt, Brace & World, 1960.

John S. Saloma, III, *Congress and the New Politics*. Little, Brown, 1969.

Robert Sherrill, "Why We Can't Depend on Congress to Keep Congress Honest." *New York Times Magazine*, July 19, 1970, pp. 5ff.

Donald E. Stokes and Warren E. Miller, "Party Government and the Salience of Congress." *Public Opinion Quarterly*, 1962, 26:531–546.

John L. Sullivan and Robert E. O'Connor, "Electoral Choice and Popular Control of Public Policy: The Case of the 1966 House Elections." *American Political Science Review*, 1972, 66:1256–1268.

U.S. Congress, House Select Committee on Committees, *Committee Organization in the House*, 3 vols. Government Printing Office, 1973.

U.S. Congress, "Committee Reform Amendments of 1974." *Report* of the Select Committee on Committees of the House of Representatives, Government Printing Office, 1974.

Index

6 7 479